INTERIOR DESIGN SECRETS

How to create a professional interior design for your home

Dedication:

This is dedicated to my father who passed away while I was writing this and never saw me become a published author. I miss his wit, and laughter and love him still.

INTERIOR
DESIGN
Secrets

How to create a professional interior design for your home

DEBORAH HEATH

Interior Design Secrets
How to create a professional interior design for your home

First published in 2015 by

Panoma Press Ltd
48 St Vincent Drive, St Albans, Herts, AL1 5SJ, UK
info@panomapress.com
www.panomapress.com

Printed in Malta by Melita Press

Book layout by Michael Inns
Artwork by Karen Gladwell

ISBN 978-1-909623-54-5

Contents

Acknowledgements

I would like to acknowledge Daniel and Andrew Priestley and Mindy Gibbins-Klein for introducing me to the concept of writing a book. It had never occurred to me that this was something I could do. Their belief, encouragement and gentle pressure kept the book alive.

I would like to acknowledge Judy Dendy who expertly took my manuscript, gave it structure and shape, asked all the right questions and brought flow and coherence to all my ideas.

I would like to acknowledge my husband for his constructive criticism on the initial manuscript and his constant love and support throughout.

I would like to thank my clients for allowing me to photograph their homes and include them in my book. It is their gratitude that makes all that I do worthwhile.

Foreword

This book was written in response to my clients' questions about the interior design process and some of the challenges that they had faced. Any major interior design project can be both daunting and exciting and the key to its success is following a design process that starts with careful planning and well thought out objectives. It is similar to going on a journey, if you don't know where you are going or don't have the route worked out you might arrive at the wrong place. So it is with Interior Design, the project starts long before anything is purchased.

It is very rewarding creating your own beautiful home and dreams really can come true. We have helped many clients create fabulous homes from relatively small design projects through to complete home renovation and this book is a distillation of our knowledge and experience with all types of properties. This book will be a source of inspiration, a guide and reference to accompany you on your design journey. Be inspired.

About the Author

As a child it was my burning ambition to become a ballet dancer and choreographer, I loved everything about the theatre not just the dancing it was the fantasy world that could be created just from someone's imagination. I didn't fulfill that ambition taking a more cerebral career instead which would give me financial security. My corporate world came to an end when my second child was born and with my husband's career taking him away from home I found balancing home, family and career an impossible life to keep in balance.

My world changed beyond recognition from managing a large financial team and dealing with business issues to looking after two babies. I returned to my more creative side and when my children were young I painted characters on the walls of the nursery, playroom and their bedrooms. Friends loved them so I was commissioned to paint for them too and naturally they would ask how to furnish the room to complement the murals. I decided to attend a short interior design course so that I could give good advice.

However I loved the course so much that I then enrolled in a 2 year part-time course in interior design and a 2 year part-time course in design and textiles. I also worked for an interior designer and had decided to start my own business when my husband announced we were moving to Madrid with his work.

This was a fantastic experience, I learnt to speak fluent Spanish, met some great people and took on some interior design commissions for some ex-pats. We moved back to England after 3 years in Madrid and I started my interior design business.

Since then I have built up my business with a large variety of clients from a 17th century cottage, barn conversion, listed Elizabethan home, to a modern property with six bedrooms on three floors. I have created designs for every room in the house for a wide range of tastes and styles. I love my work as no two jobs are the same, they all have their unique challenges and I get to meet some wonderful people. My passion is that I believe that everyone can have a beautifully designed house. I have loved developing my business using all the skills I learnt in the corporate world together with a lot more acquired as a mother. As the children got older I was able to dedicate more time to my business and now with both of them at university I have been able to give it all my focus and attention and recently won an award from the International Property Awards for Interior Design Private Residence South East UK. I now have a small team of dedicated and enthusiastic designers that has allowed Design by Deborah Ltd to expand into the successful company it is today.

I still love to dance, I regularly go to dance classes and I am choreographer to a local amateur dramatic group. I now create a theatre of a kind for my clients which gives them the perfect backdrop to enhance the quality of their lives.

Contact:
Deborah@Designbydeborah.co.uk
Designbydeborah.co.uk

Introduction

Do you need an Interior Designer? Of course you do, yes. Can you be your own Interior Designer? Why not! All those beautiful homes that you have admired have one thing in common, they have been thoughtfully and carefully planned. They don't happen by accident, someone had a vision and that someone could be you.

This book gives you the steps you need to take to create the home of your dreams. If you have ever visualised how your home could look then this book will help you make it a reality. The fact that you are reading this book has already meant you have taken the first step.

I was inspired to write this by my clients. Many of them ask for my help because they have got lost in the process by focusing on the detail long before they have thought about designing the space from the top. The choices become a lot easier when you have clearly thought through what you are going to do with the space.

- Never again walk into a fabric shop not knowing where to start, overwhelmed by the choice, hoping that a piece of fabric will jump out at you and inspire your creative juices. *Chapter 1* shows you where to start with your interior design ideas.

- Never again walk down the high street with your partner, hoping you will both fall in love with the same thing, disappointed that it doesn't happen. *Chapter 2* shows you how to plan more effectively, avoiding all those difficult shopping trips.

- Never again put yourself under unnecessary stress and time pressure to make those important decisions about your home, and never again compromise on your dreams and vision. *Chapter 3* shows you how to gather your ideas, *Chapter 4* helps you with deciding what is suitable and appropriate.

- Worried about what goes with what? What colour to paint the walls, will it all be too dark, and what kind of lighting should you have? *Chapter 5* helps you understand the combining of colour, pattern and fabrics; *Chapter 6* helps you understand the impact of light and lighting.

- Will it all fit together? Is the sofa too big? What kind of curtains to have? How can you use what you have to best effect? Be one step ahead and learn about the key elements of scale proportion, balance, focal point and harmony. *Chapter 7* teaches you the design principles that the professionals use. *Chapter 8* helps you add the finishing touches, the lamps, the rugs, and the right kind of curtains.

Does all this sound familiar? Don't make those expensive mistakes and find yourself living with something you don't like but is too expensive to change.

This book is not so much about showing you styles and giving you examples that you can copy, but more about how to develop your own particular style and translate it into your home.

There are so many factors that affect an interior that it is almost impossible to duplicate exactly somebody else's home and style and it is often not successful. It is much more fun creating your own interior design scheme.

Some of today's interior design schemes are expensive, bland and conformist. Try not to copy a mixture of "high-end developer" with "international hotel lobby" and create something soulless or replicate show homes that are clearly shop windows. It is a shame that so many people believe that their interiors should look like penthouse service apartments kitted out from a catalogue.

The interior design of a private home needs to be comfortable, practical and loved by its owners. The design needs to acknowledge the age and architecture of the building and reflect the taste, possessions and experiences of the people who live there. So there is no "one size fits all" solution to redesigning your home.

1

Establishing your rationale

Why are you doing this design project? What do you want to achieve? This seems like an obvious question but unless you have a clear idea of your basic objective you are going to find it really difficult to move the process forward. To help you clarify your thoughts, here are some questions that will help you focus on the outcome.

Is it simply to prepare the house for sale?

This may seem an unlikely reason to embark on any redesign work, but it can greatly enhance your chances of not only selling but also achieving a good price. The investment in updating the property can be more than compensated by the higher sales price. The important point to remember is that any prospective buyers need to be able to imagine themselves and their things in your property. The best way to achieve this is by de-personalising and de-cluttering. We could all de-clutter at some time or another, but there will never be a better time than when you are going to move house. You want to expand the visual space, decorate with neutral tones and it will appeal to a large group of house buyers. They need to easily see themselves living there.

It can be a great way to mark a new direction in your life.

Have you had a change in your life circumstances?

Life doesn't stand still and is continually changing and developing and we need our homes to meet our needs. It may be you have just started a family, or your youngest child has just left home. You may now need to look after elderly relatives or your caring role is no longer required. Perhaps you have started a business and you are working from home or the nature of your work means you entertain a lot. Maybe you have just started a new relationship or one has just ended. Whatever your personal circumstances are it can be a great way to mark a new direction in your life by taking on the challenge of an interior design project.

Interior Design Secrets . . . .

Do you simply want to update out of date or tired décor?

No matter how clean and tidy we are, colours fade, fabrics become grubby and out of fashion, carpets wear and woodwork gets knocked. It is often the case that once you start on a project in one part of the house you quickly want to improve other areas, so be prepared for a roll-out of many interior design projects.

Do you need to create more space?

For many people it is more economical or practical to create more space within their home than to move house. This could be an extension, conservatory or a loft conversion. You may wish to build over existing single storey buildings, convert a garage, shed or basement. There are prefabricated buildings that can be erected or it can be designed and built on site. In all these circumstances you will need to have access to professional help. You probably also need to apply for some form of planning permission, and the impact on your project of costs (not only of the

Before and after

Colours and styles in interior design go in and out of fashion just as they do with clothes, this is the same window redecorated 20 years later.

application but also the subsequent building inspections) and the time required should not be underestimated. Your local planning office will be able to give you the appropriate advice. If your neighbours have already done something similar, then start by talking to them and ask them all those important questions. Most likely they will be happy to tell you about planning, limitations imposed by the authorities and their overall experience and advice. This sort of information is priceless and a great way to get to know the neighbours.

Do you want to use the space you have more effectively?

You may not want to add space but use the space you have more effectively. Perhaps change the room's function for example from a dining room into a playroom or a spare bedroom into a study. You may want to create more visual space by removing internal walls and develop an open plan living space. It is important before removing any internal walls that professional advice is sought. What may seem like an internal hollow wall may have some weight bearing brick pillars. Any change to the structure of the property will also need a type of planning permission based on a structural survey. This should be seen as insurance as a professional building inspector is responsible for making sure your house doesn't collapse.

Below
Children's bedrooms are one area where careful consideration needs to be given in how the space is going to be used and how best to achieve it.

Interior Design Secrets . . . .

What might constrain you?

There may well be other factors to think of before starting your detailed planning? The starting point should always be what you would ideally like before determining whether it is feasible and how much it would cost. There are always limiting factors, which might be physical or monetary, however without developing your ideal design you don't know how much of the dream you actually can have. Perhaps more than you had realised.

Adding extra rooms is often one of the main reasons for embarking on a major re-design of a home. Our family lives are far more complicated than ever before with caring for elderly parents, children staying at home longer before leaving and step families that may only live with you for part of the week. Living space needs to be flexible and may need to perform more than one function. The planning of these rooms needs to be carefully thought through, examining the range of options that your particular property allows. Optimum space planning is a science, and done well will have a true effect on the way you lead your lives. Sacrificing space that performs one function to relieve another where there is a lot of pressure can bring great rewards without embarking on a large building programme. If you are unsure what to do for the best then seek professional help. A good architect will look at your house as a whole and suggest the best way of utilising your space.

If you decide that the only way to have the home you want is to build, then look at all the options before obtaining quotes. If you are considering a loft conversion these are some of the things you need to consider; firstly, the pitch of your roof has to be high enough, secondly, you will loose some space in order to gain access to the loft and thirdly, if you plan to have dormer windows you will almost certainly require planning permission. Also the fire regulations change when there is a second floor. There are excellent loft conversion companies who will handle the whole process for you from planning to completion, however they won't look at other options available to you for adding space.

If you are unsure what to do for the best then seek professional help.

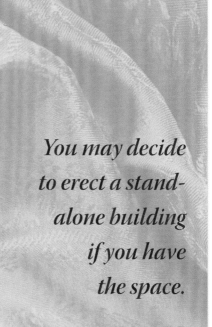

You may decide to erect a stand-alone building if you have the space.

You may decide to extend the property. Everybody should be familiar with the fact that planning is required before any work can start. However frustrating this may seem, it does protect you, your property and your community. This process varies considerably depending on where you live. If you live in a conservation area, an area of outstanding beauty or your house is listed, then this will certainly affect the process. Your architect should be fully aware of all the issues and design an extension that meets your needs and is sympathetic to the style of your home. Don't think solely about the extension as a separate entity but how it will integrate into your home. When the work has been completed do you want the extension to be an integral part of the home or a separate room or suite of rooms?

You may decide to erect a stand-alone building if you have the space. This can be an ideal solution if you are trying to create a space that you don't want to integrate into your home. You may need to accommodate an elderly relative, create a teenage den or a separate workspace. I know somebody who has his studio in the garden, dresses for work and his commute is a walk to the end of the garden. This might seem strange but it really helps him to move from home mode to work mode. There are obviously factors that need to be considered, such as planning, supply of services and some sort of firm base needs to be created. However there are many companies that can supply a prefabricated building in any style, and this can be a quick solution to pressing space needs. I highly recommend you discuss this option with an architect or engineer to give you an objective opinion.

All these options should be considered and information is plentiful in publications, on the Internet and advertisements. However there is no substitute for professional help. Most professional people will have an initial discussion with you for free and will be able to advise you who it is best to talk to. Be wary of the builder who tells you that you do not need to talk to an architect, surveyor or engineer. You will need to do your homework to ensure you get the right kind of help and your local council can give you impartial advice. There are fees involved but they are trained specialists who have professional indemnity insurance so that if they do give you incorrect advice you will have some recourse. They can independently advise on all your options; they can give you some idea of overall costs and may even be happy to recommend companies that you should ask to quote. Remember your home is probably your most valuable asset so anything you do to it should enhance that investment.

The final choice is to move house. Sometimes this is the only option if you need to move to another location. However it is worth considering even when looking to upsize or downsize your property. I know somebody who did a house swap in the same village. They were a young family looking for more space and the other homeowner lived on her own and needed less space. There are obviously significant costs involved and this often puts people off, but don't underestimate the stress and costs in major building work.

Where not to start – common mistakes

Resist the temptation to start with the fabric!

This is such a common mistake. I quite often go to meet a client who has a large collection of fabric samples and they are completely confused about which to start with. They just can't seem to find the *right* one. That is because they don't really know what fabric they are looking for. You can bet that they haven't created a plan or mood board! You'll read about this in Chapter 3.

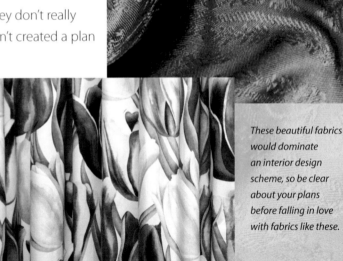

I like to think of it as the same as choosing your earrings before you have chosen the outfit you wish to wear. It is doing things back to front. Once you have bought the outfit you may well change your mind about the earrings and this is the same with choosing the fabric first. Have you ever bought metres of fabric on impulse hoping to use it in a scheme one day but it is still in its bag in a cupboard somewhere? If you have fallen in love with a particular piece of fabric it may restrict your thinking and not allow you to make the most of all your other choices.

These beautiful fabrics would dominate an interior design scheme, so be clear about your plans before falling in love with fabrics like these.

A well-designed room is never based just on one fabric; it will be a combination of fabrics and all the other elements, which will make your home look fabulous.

The problem is, and I completely understand, that looking at fabrics is the fun part of creating a design. If you have ever walked around an exhibition, or a fabric shop you will have seen the fantastic range of fabrics that are now available, for some it creates inspiration, for others confusion. However without knowing in what direction your design is going, it is impossible to know where to start looking so you will probably be drawn to the colours and patterns that you would normally choose. As a result, this can prevent you from being open minded about everything else available.

In Chapter 5 we will look at how to choose the colour and pattern of the fabrics that work well together to create an exciting and interesting scheme.

Seduced by the Sales!

So many of us wait for the very well advertised sales before we go to the shops to make a significant furniture, fabric or lighting purchase. We wait to see what they have reduced before we decide what we are going to buy.

Most shops sell commodities, not a service, they want to sell something to you so they can clear space for the new deliveries. The showroom is designed to show everything at its best and the salesmen are trained to sell.

So STOP!

Are you really going to let the shop decide what is going to be in your home? Is it the right colour? Does it fit? How will it look with everything else you have? Can you really make that decision in the showroom?

So often a bargain in the sales ends up being an expensive mistake; which you may not be able to correct immediately. Don't do it. Make sure you are in control of what you buy. Whilst buying items in the sales that you want and need can certainly save you money, make sure you know exactly what you are looking for before you enter the showroom. You are far less likely to be persuaded to buy something you don't need.

Of course sales are no longer restricted to particular times of the year anymore, there are always special offers to be taken advantage of and even if there aren't any

So often a bargain in the sales ends up being an expensive mistake.

advertised you can often negotiate a discount with the store manager. So don't feel the pressure to make that important purchasing decision within the advertised sales window, it is just a marketing tool.

So how do you avoid being seduced by the sales and all the hype that surrounds these heavily advertised events. Plan, plan and plan. It sounds boring and tedious but it doesn't have to be. We will look at how to draw up your plan in Chapter 2. The best way to visualise how anything is going to look within your home is to create a mood board. We will look at how to do this in Chapter 3.

What you <u>should</u> be thinking through carefully

The "unknowns"

There are always unknowns when taking on a project. All major house renovation projects should come with a health warning.

"It will be more complicated, take longer, cost more than you had originally anticipated."

Why am I telling you all this? So that you can be prepared. A large building project will take over your life for a period of time and can create a lot of stress and you do not want it to be a disappointment. Problems need to be seen as challenges to be overcome and some you can anticipate and plan for and others will need to be negotiated as they arise. Nothing is impossible and there will always be somebody who will be able to help you. On that positive note I have outlined below some of the common challenges that can occur and how best to plan and deal with them before embarking on such an undertaking.

Being thorough with budgets and quotes

Establishing your budget is key to the successful completion of any project. Do not start something you can't afford. You only have to see some of those reality television programmes on interior design to know that costs only go one way.

Selecting whom you are going to work with, gathering quotes and agreeing timetables is an important process. References need to be followed up and take a look at some of their previous work.

"It will be more complicated, take longer, cost more than you had originally anticipated."

Make sure you regularly communicate with your builder and other tradespeople.

Being clear about responsibilities, communication and decisions

- **Project management:** establish who is responsible for the different areas of the work, in particular what you are responsible for.

- **Decision making:** there are always critical decisions to be made before a project can progress so make sure you know what they are and give yourself enough time to consider all your options and be aware of the critical time path. Planning is the key.

- **Identify suppliers:** suppliers of either goods or services need to be chosen and organised well in advance, this is because various trades depend on each other completing certain tasks and having access to the right products to ensure everything keeps to timetable as much as possible.

- **Communication:** make sure you regularly communicate with your builder and other tradespeople, the quicker any problems are resolved the less of an impact it will have on your design scheme.

- **Contingencies:** both cost and time must be built into the schedule. If you have no contingency you risk not being able to complete the work.

Allow time for planning permission

Planning issues can cause delays and it is always worth using an architect or builder who has experience in negotiating with your local planning department. Although rules and regulations should be consistent across all councils, it doesn't quite work like that in practice.

Give yourself plenty of time to go through the planning process and discuss your plans with your neighbours. Your neighbours have the right to object and they are more likely to be sympathetic to your needs if you have discussed it with them first and listened to their objections if they have any. They may only be worried about the impact on them during the building work and if you can accommodate all their concerns then they are less likely to object.

The planning process is there to ensure that not only has the building been designed to meet all the building regulations and is in keeping with its environment but that it also stipulates the inspections required throughout the construction. They are there to protect you and to ensure that the construction is meeting all the necessary regulations. If the inspector is not happy about something then he may request additional information, for example deeper foundations and soil samples. The inspector will not sign off a stage in the building construction unless he is satisfied and the builder cannot move on to the next stage until he has been given authority to do so.

If your home is listed or in a conservation area then the planning process will be more complicated and you may need specialist advice. The planners will want to ensure that the integrity of the building is maintained and may request additional inspections, specify certain materials and prevent modern techniques from being used. There are specialist architects and builders who deal with such properties and should be able to help you through the process. Investment in expert advice at the beginning may well pay dividends later in the project.

Give yourself plenty of time to go through the planning process.

Further considerations when enlarging your property

When you are adding accommodation you are generally adding to the load of existing systems. Most houses are not built with spare capacity on their electrical and plumbing systems so they need to be checked. Extra radiators or another shower may put undue pressure on your existing boiler and therefore for the whole building to run more efficiently you may need to replace it, and that needs to be built into your plan and costs. Increasing the number of lights and sockets may overload a fuse board and you may need to upgrade. Talk to plumbers and electricians before you start planning seriously to make sure your home can support any new systems you may require.

This pre-planning is important to avoid disasters that can happen once the work has started. For example you may find you don't have enough pressure from your water or gas, or that the wiring in the house is in a desperate need of replacing. These are costly, time consuming and messy tasks but don't cut corners with the electrics or plumbing. It isn't worth it. You want to be safe and free from disasters and certain that the improvements you are making to your property are certified, work well and are fully insured. An electrician can close your house down if he feels that the electrics are unsafe. It is always worth giving the main systems a health check before embarking on any major project.

RIGHT:

Before and after

This bathroom went through a significant makeover to make it more in keeping with the 300 year old cottage.

Interior Design Secrets . . . .

Why are you doing this design project? Be clear on your rationale as this will govern the amount of time, energy and money you want to invest.

What are your physical and financial constraints? A touch of realism will prevent you from overstretching yourself.

Start your interior design scheme with a plan rather than with the fabric. Choosing the detail too early can end up as a distraction.

Do not go shopping in the sales without a clear idea of what you want to buy. Only then is it a true bargain.

Be prepared. Give yourself plenty of time to pursue any planning permission you may need and give your home an M.O.T.

Ask your electrician and plumber to look at your current facilities and to check whether they can take any more capacity.

Your Interior Design journey starts here

HOT TIPS

2

Capture your enthusiasm

Remember how you felt when you first saw your property? When we first move in to a new home we are bubbling over with enthusiasm. We have grand ideas of how we want to use the space, the colours, the fabrics, the style and feel, with little effort we are able to feel how this new home will look. But too often we haven't the time, money or resources to do anything about it straight away. So we leave it until some other goal that we have set ourselves is achieved and then we will do it!

Sadly many people all too quickly adopt the previous owner's home style. They hang pictures on picture hooks that have been left in the wall. The hated curtains stay longer than they should because after a while you are so used to seeing them they no longer offend. The previously fashionable paint effects and colours just get absorbed into your home life. The problem with this is your house hasn't become your home. Do you find yourself apologising when guests come round because you see your house through their eyes and you tell them of your plans to redecorate the Barbie pink guest bedroom they will be staying in?

Even if time and money are an issue initially you should capitalise on your early creative senses. It doesn't take any money and only a little time to pull together some ideas, even if you are unable to action them straight away. Once you have made up your mind that you need to take action, you will start to notice not only what you need to change in your own home, but also how your friends' and families' homes are decorated. This can be fun and often inspiring – it helps you decide what you want, and what you don't want.

What would you like to change? If you are planning to completely refurbish your house as one complete project, then not only do you need to have a very well thought through plan of action, you may also need to plan to move out of the property for a while. This is especially true if you are going to be losing water or electricity for significant periods of time, let alone if walls and roofs are being removed or replaced. It will also allow for the project to progress much quicker.

Are you planning to refurbish only one room or are you going to make your way around the house a room at a time. If you are intending to tackle each room one after another then how do you choose where to start? My advice would be to start in the room from which you will get most benefit either because it will improve your wellbeing or will function far more effectively, this is usually the busiest room in the house. If you start in the spare bedroom, what normally happens is you run out of steam before you get too far through the house and you put off tackling the complex rooms.

Strike while the iron is hot and you are full of enthusiasm. Start with the most important room that needs to be refurbished and that will give you the best return for your efforts.

If you are intending to tackle each room one after another then how do you choose where to start?

The different kinds of plan

Once you are clear about your reasons for re-designing your home and have a sense of the look you want to achieve, now is the time to start putting all your ideas on to paper. Then you can explore your various options and start to evaluate them. You need to have a good idea of how you are going to use the space and through the process of planning you will be able to see how the room will function. This is less creative than looking at colours and fabrics but is an important first step and gives context to all your ideas.

The kitchen is usually the hub of the house so invest time and effort in getting it right.

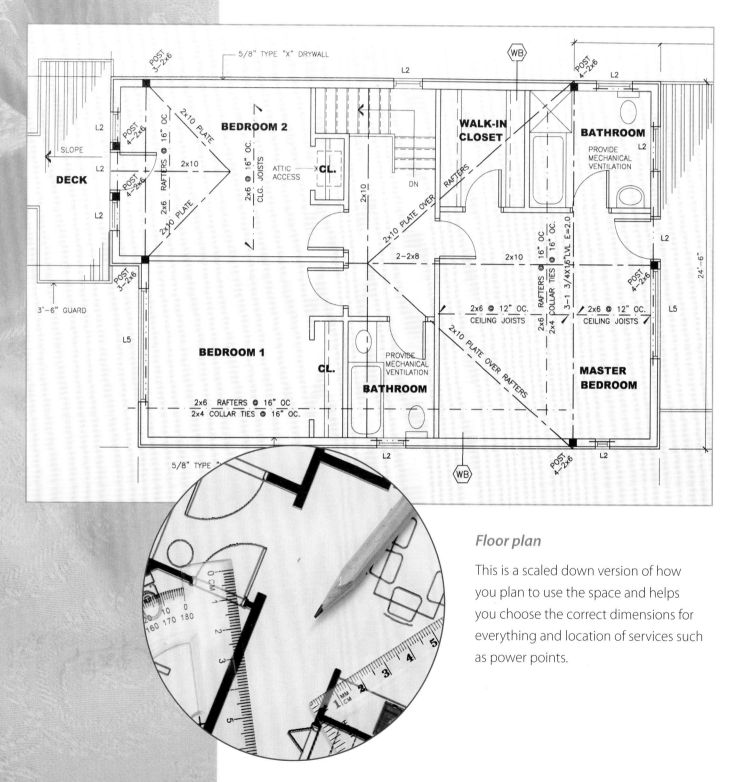

5/8" TYPE "X" DRYWALL

POST 3—2x6

POST 4—2x6

L2

SLOPE

POST 4—2x6

L2

POST 4—2x6

DECK

2x10 PLATE

RAFTERS @ 16" OC.

2x10

2x10 PLATE

2x10 PLATE

BEDROOM 2

2x6 @ 16" OC.

CLG. JOISTS

ATTIC ACCESS

CL.

2x10

L2

DN

WALK-IN CLOSET

2x10 PLATE OVER RAFTERS

WB

POST 4—2x6

L2

BATHROOM

PROVIDE MECHANICAL VENTILATION

L2

L2

POST 3—2x6

3'—6" GUARD

L5

2—2x8

2x10

RAFTERS @ 16" OC.

2x4 COLLAR TIES @ 16" OC.

3—1 3/4x16"LVL E=2.0

2x6 @ 12" OC.
CEILING JOISTS

2x6 @ 12" OC.
CEILING JOISTS

L5

POST 4—2x6

24'—6"

BEDROOM 1

CL.

2x10 PLATE OVER RAFTERS

PROVIDE MECHANICAL VENTILATION

BATHROOM

MASTER BEDROOM

2x6 RAFTERS @ 16" OC.
2x4 COLLAR TIES @ 16" OC.

5/8" TYPE "

L2

WB

POST 4—2x6

L2

Floor plan

This is a scaled down version of how you plan to use the space and helps you choose the correct dimensions for everything and location of services such as power points.

Interior Design Secrets . . . .

Project plan

This gives you an idea of how long all the different tasks that are necessary to complete your plan will take. Always build in a contingency. This plan will form the basis of the discussion with the builder allowing for far more accurate quotes with far fewer extras being added at the end of the project.

	Task	Assigned To	Start	End	Dur	2015											
						Jan	Feb	Mar	Apr	May	Jun	Jul	Aug	Sep	Oct	Nov	Dec
1	Contract Writing		1/20/15	12/14/15	236												
2	Contract Signing		1/20/15	3/3/15	31												
3	Secure Financing		2/15/15	3/27/15	30												
4	Review Tenders		3/14/15	4/25/15	31												
5	Obtain Permits		4/9/15	5/18/15	30												
6	Site Work		4/30/15	8/31/15	89												
7	Plumbing		7/21/15	10/16/15	61												
8	Electrical		8/6/15	10/30/15	61												
9	Roof		8/21/15	12/7/15	78												
10	Inspection		11/5/15	12/14/15	30												
11	Move In		12/1/15	12/4/15	1												

Mood board

This provides a home for all those ideas, samples, pictures you have been collating. This will eventually be honed down to all the items you plan to have in your design scheme.

Budget

All the tasks that are to be performed and all the items you wish to buy have a cost so this information will come from your project plan and mood board.

The important thing about planning is that your plans are continually refined as you make decisions, receive quotes and refine your design scheme. Then you will be in control.

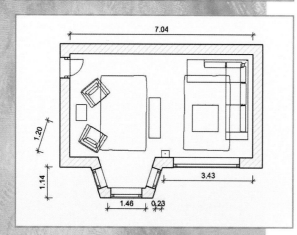

Creating a floor plan

How is the space going to be used?

Firstly and very importantly, knowing what you want to achieve with your interior design does mean asking yourself how is the space to be used? It is all too easy to accept the layout of the rooms that have been inherited. Is the room dedicated to one function or is to be used in a variety of ways, maybe at different times of the day? A study may become a television room for the children in the evening. Do you have hobbies or interests that need a dedicated space, for example a music room? When you are planning, think long-term. Is the pressure you have on space relatively short-term? Or are you anticipating a need for space relatively soon. There are many ways to accommodate more than one function, for example, add a sofa bed in the playroom for when guests visit. You may want to introduce a bureau in the lounge to allow for a workstation, or a bunk bed with a desk underneath for a place to do homework.

These will all feed into your floor plan. The most important thing in planning is accommodating your future needs and this may need physical alterations to the room, for example power points, Internet access, relocating radiators or lighting. A floor plan allows you to visualise how the space could work for you and consider a number of options. There are web sites that allow you to download (free of charge) basic drawing tools that will allow you to create your own floor plans and clearly review how the space should be organised. Here are some examples, **Smartdraw. com**, **Edrawsoft.com** and **Homestyler.com** There are other web sites and apps available and whichever you choose will depend on how easy you find they are to use. There is always a trade off between ease of use and flexibility of options.

When you plan the position of the furniture especially, think about how the room is accessed, how much space do you need around the furniture and how much furniture do you need. You should also think about where you turn the light on and off, exiting and entering, space for the door to fully open, space for access to any cupboards or drawers, you will be amazed at how many times I have seen this as a problem. Believe me, there is no point buying a cupboard if you cannot get proper access to it, you simply won't use it.

Above

Here are two alternative floor plans for the same room. The long thin rectangle is a unit for the television and its position would determine all the electric and satellite points.

Who uses the space?

There is always a balance between what is beautiful and what is practical. A deep pile cream carpet in the lounge may be beautiful, but if you have young children and pets it is probably not practical. This beautiful room needs to stay looking beautiful so don't plan for a space that would be difficult for you to maintain. Your new home should liberate you not enslave you. A well-designed space that suits all those that use it can be both practical and beautiful.

When you are considering who uses the space, does this include guests? Are you able to dedicate a space for this and is it important to be able to create a good impression? This is becoming increasingly true for those who now work from home and may choose to hold meetings or entertain there. The planning of this space is very important and the style of the room needs to reflect the image you want to portray. Your style plan will be your mood board or style board, which we look at in the next chapter.

What will you need to buy?

Your floor plan will allow you to identify exactly what you need to buy and the range of measurements before you go anywhere near a shop. Shopping is exhausting if you haven't identified your parameters and even more so if you are buying with a partner. Often arguments ensue because you are not sure what you are looking for, you can't agree on what you like and worst of all, you finally buy something that you both find least offensive. A compromise which neither of you really like, so you both are unhappy. Then when you get home you realise the sofa won't fit, the chosen bedroom furniture probably won't go up your stairs, or the light in the hallway will hang too low. The excitement about redecorating your home starts to become a frustrating problem that you can't agree on. The most expensive thing about interior design are the things that are bought in haste, often under time pressure but are then too expensive to replace even though they don't look right. A well thought through plan will help avoid this.

Your new home should liberate you not enslave you.

Creating a project plan

Creating a project plan sounds obvious but most people don't do it. It takes time; you may well know what you are doing so why bother. If you don't have a project plan it can cost you more time and money in the long run. If you don't have a project plan you can miss important tasks.

The knock-on effects

Often when you are making changes it has knock-on effects elsewhere, for example if the way the door opens has altered, does that affect where the light switch should be, and at what point do you ask the electrician to accommodate that? If the television is to move to another place in the lounge what about the aerial connection? Or if the position of the dining table changes what about the pendant light if it no longer hangs above it? Radiators will need to be planned too – where will they go and how will they fit in with the furniture you plan to include, and at what point you need the plumber to install them? Even if you are aware of issues like these, have you built them into your schedule? What if the engineer can't come out for two weeks, the electrician isn't free for another month, without a plan these seemingly minor points can have a major effect on the overall timetable. You will not want to be putting up wallpaper until the light switch has moved for example.

Below you can see how two simple tasks have been set out with a breakdown of what's involved and when it needs to be done.

Often when you are making changes it has knock-on effects elsewhere.

Task	Week 1	Week 2	Week 3	Week 4
Bathroom Radiator				
Decide location	▬			
Gather quotes from plumbers	▬			
Agree cost and date for work		▬		
Choose design		▬		
Choose colour		▬		
Order radiator		▬		
Clear bathroom			▬	
Decorate behind radiator location				▬

Task	Week 1	Week 2	Week 3	Week 4
Hallway Blind				
Choose style of blind	▨			
Choose fabric	▨			
Gather quotes from curtain makers		▨		
Agree costs		▨		
Agree date for delivery of blind		▨		
Organise painting of hallway			▨	
Install blind				▨

A project plan also helps you to control costs. By sitting down and methodically going through a plan of action you will identify all the steps you need to take and will be able to quantify the costs. Therefore if for some reason the plan changes it is easier to track how it is going to impact on your plan and cost.

Who is responsible for what?

When you are pulling together your project plan you need to identify who is responsible for organising which tasks. Whilst you are project manager, the builder will also be organising his team of workmen and you need to clearly identify where his job finishes. For example is he doing the painting and decorating or installing the kitchen or fitted furniture or are you organising that separately. The bigger the project the more complicated it is but your builder or architect should be happy to give you advice on all the different aspects of the project you need to have considered.

Your various plans allow you to share your thoughts with everyone else in the family. They can contribute their ideas and they will feel involved and avoid misunderstandings, especially on those important shopping trips. Any major work will also affect them. Firstly are they able to help, maybe with decluttering? They may have strong feelings about the timings, holiday plans, exam timetables or heavy workload, something you may have not thought about. All these factors are so much easier to build into your plans if they have been written down.

The bigger the project the more complicated it is.

Preparing your project plan

How do you prepare your project plan? This need not be too difficult if you approach it in a logical manner. The plan does not need to be a professional looking document. So if you prefer to hand write it that's fine or you may prefer to create a spread sheet on a computer where it is easier to update.

Where do you start?

The start point should be to list all the tasks that need to be performed and have a cost. A task maybe to choose a fabric, or request quotes, or when you need to place an order for a carpet, or to contact the planning office. There needs to be a list of actions that someone has to perform in order for the project to progress smoothly, and that includes decisions. You should list whatever you need to keep track of in order to keep control of the project. You may want to produce a list by room or by type of activity for example lighting or building work, in other words whatever works best for you. Go into as much detail as you can. You will find that the list grows the more you think about your plan and you will probably have many iterations of it before you have covered everything.

Initially the data will be a guess of target dates and estimated costs, then as you get firm quotes you will be able to be more accurate. This is a working document and needs to be continually updated as the project develops and information changes. Thus in one place you will be able to see how long the project will take, how much it will cost, what needs to be done when and the impact any changes will have. If you have employed a professional project manager he would have a sophisticated system, which essentially would do the same thing. It is a small investment in time and if you are not happy producing something like this, then delegate it to someone else.

> *You should list whatever you need to keep track of in order to keep control of the project.*

Who will manage the project?

This may seem an odd item to include in a book about interior design. However creating the design is only part of the process and managing the project afterwards is equally as important. It is probably fair to say that a majority of building projects overrun both in time and cost. It can be for many reasons, some of which are unavoidable but there are others that aren't, such as orders not being placed in a timely manner, incorrect items supplied, important parts missing, tradesmen not being available when needed and any one of these can have a large knock-on effect as it throws out the timing of everything else. There are factors that can't be avoided such as the weather or structural problems that are unknown until the skeleton of the building has been revealed; however they still need managing. It is important that everyone involved with the work knows who will make the key decisions and when they need to be made. This person needs to be able to respond quickly and with authority. If the decision-making process is slow and confusing then this will have a large impact on the smooth running and potentially the cost of the project.

It is probably fair to say that a majority of building projects overrun both in time and cost.

The professional project manager

There is always the option of using a professional project manager. This should be a serious consideration if you are not living on site or you are not able to visit daily. Architects, surveyors, structural engineers are ideal for major construction work and interior designers are best for interior transformations, or you may choose to involve a combination of these professions. It is not unusual for an architect to work closely with an interior designer. There is obviously a cost involved but this needs to be compared with the benefit of avoiding a delayed project or incorrect decisions being made by the builder or other tradesmen. The cost of delay can be significant, especially if you are renting somewhere whilst the work is being carried out.

The appointed project manager will produce a schedule of works, which everyone agrees to and lays out all the tasks and their associated timings. Unless you understand the complexities of construction and all the regulations that need to be met you may find it difficult to produce a plan at this level of detail. This will also take into account all the necessary building control inspections. The added benefit is that they will control the scheduled payments ensuring that this happens at an agreed point in the process. This also helps to avoid misunderstandings or disputes with the builder. The other significant advantage of having a project manager is that they have the knowledge and experience to be able to resolve problems quickly. It is unrealistic to think that in any large building project there won't be any problems, however it is how these are dealt with that will determine how they affect the overall project.

A professional project manager will have access to resources and information not generally available and this is how they justify their fees. You may even be able to agree a penalty clause if the project overruns or introduce a bonus if delivered ahead of schedule. This can certainly focus everyone's minds. This type of control is probably over the top for purely a redecoration, but I would recommend considering it if building work is involved.

Putting together your own plan

The majority of small projects are self-managed and this can be very rewarding as you see your ideas come to life. It can also be very frustrating so you need to use your plan to create a very clear job specification. The **Homebuilding.co.uk** website has a great example of a project planner. **Excellencegateway.org.uk** gives a very clear example of how to construct a gantt chart*. **Projectsmart.co.uk**, contains project management templates and tools which you can download for a small charge. **Yourbuildplan.co.uk** helps you create a build plan strategy and guides you through the process from planning to choosing and managing your builder.

Of course you can simply create your own spreadsheet, don't worry if you are unsure about using the correct terminology, so long as your plan is written clearly, everyone should fully understand what is required.

* Gantt charts illustrate the start and finish dates of the terminal elements
   and summary elements of a project.

The majority of small projects are self-managed and this can be very rewarding as you see your ideas come to life.

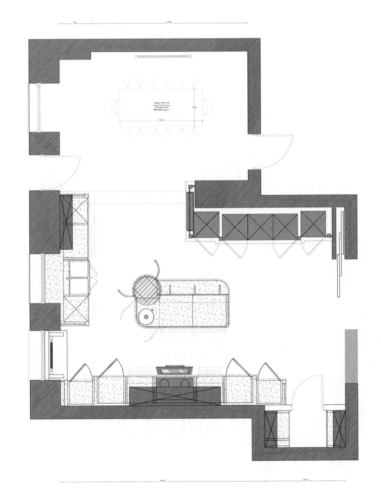

Implementing the project plan

The project plan will form the basis of the discussion with the builder allowing for far more accurate quotes with far fewer extras being added at the end of the project and it will be easier to compare quotes. Try not to use any ambiguous terms or be too vague. If there are certain areas that you have yet to make a decision about then make this clear in the plan. Never assume that a builder will know exactly what you want him to do unless you tell him. For example if you ask the builder to remove a wooden floor he will not assume that he is replacing it unless you have requested him to do so and he won't have included it in his price.

If there are certain areas that you have yet to make a decision about then make this clear in the plan.

Don't underestimate the amount of time involved in managing your projects.

More complex projects

With more complex design projects you will almost certainly be employing a number of different people and it will help their working relationship if they all understand your project plan and the final objective from the start. Don't underestimate the amount of time involved in managing such an undertaking and you may find it useful to put some time in the diary on a regular basis that says 'review project status'. This will give you time to monitor the progress, discuss any difficulties with the builder, and make any adjustments to the plan as necessary. You may find that you need to delay the decorator, re-schedule the electrician or re-organise delivery of a piece of furniture.

The plan needs to have a timeline, as can be seen in the examples, that is realistic and that all parties feel is achievable. This will make it much easier to keep track of the progress of your scheme. A plan becomes even more important if in order to create your design scheme you will be losing the use of certain facilities such as heating, hot water or telecommunications or access to a room especially a kitchen or a bathroom. You should give some thought to how you will cope if for some reason you are without important facilities longer that you had planned.

If you are dealing with a lot of different tradesmen then identify within each team who the key people are that you will receive and give updates to. Agree on the best form of communication whether it is email, text, phone call or social media to ensure that there is no time wasted in messages not being picked up. Remember that the best tradesmen are always busy and are often booked for months in advance, so to make sure that the completion of your interior design scheme isn't delayed it is best to make a provisional booking with them explaining that when the project is under way you will have a more accurate idea of exactly when you will be ready to employ them.

There is nothing more frustrating than nearly finishing a scheme but then having to wait for months for the decorator or curtain maker, and that is usually the part that you have looked forward to seeing most of all. This also applies to ordering any materials when you are asking for quotes from suppliers ask them about availability and stock levels. If stock levels are low and you have a reasonably good idea of the quantity you will need but you are waiting for confirmation from someone then most suppliers will let you put a reserve on it for a limited space of time. It is also worth finding out if anything is being discontinued because if you are buying a bathroom suite for example and the toilet isn't available but you have taken delivery of the rest, you want to be sure that it is still being manufactured. Suppliers are not always good at letting you know which ranges are to be discontinued because of course they still want to sell them.

How do you choose who to work with?

It is always a difficult decision but is so important. There are many consumer web sites that can give you specific advice on how to check that all the tradespeople you wish to employ have the right qualifications, belong to the appropriate trade associations and have the correct insurance cover. Here are a few examples. **Trustmark.org.uk** is a website that lists tradesmen that have been licensed by the government and are operating within their endorsed standards. **Findacraftsman. com** is the Guild of Master Craftsmen, offering advice and a helpline on how to find reliable tradesmen. Websites like **ratedpeople.com** and **servicemagic.co.uk** rely on consumer feedback to verify quality of work. There are others but be aware that some websites are purely means of advertising.

Remember that the best tradesmen are always busy and are often booked for months in advance.

All reputable companies will be happy for you to talk to their previous clients.

Getting recommendations

The most important thing is that you do your homework. Investing time upfront in obtaining recommendations will prevent heartache further down the line in either an unfinished or badly completed project. The very worst situation you want to avoid, is employing somebody to rectify other peoples mistakes, this can be very expensive in time and money. There are many television programmes that have explored this subject and have made us all very suspicious of the building trade. They have been made for entertainment value and therefore they have selected the worst examples, but be assured there are many good, reliable tradesmen out there, you just need to make sure you use them and not the cowboys by doing your homework.

You need to select at least three companies to give you a quote. These are companies you may have done business with before, they may have been personally recommended to you or you have seen them advertising locally. If you have not worked with them before then ask to talk to previous clients and review their previous work, even if they have come personally recommended. All reputable companies will be happy for you to talk to their previous clients.

Asking the right questions

Draw up a list of key questions to ask and talk to more than one of their satisfied clients. With tradesmen you should always ask to see their insurance certificates they should have public liability, professional indemnity and employee liability cover. Find out if they are members of any trade associations and check their credentials. If they are members of a trade association this will often protect any guarantees that have been given even when the company that issued the warranty and has done the work no longer exists. Check the tradesmen's web site and any other social media activity they may have and ask for feedback about them. Involve other members of the family to help you. They may have contacts that can help with your choice.

A lot of your decision will come down to how well you think you can work with them. If everything else has checked out and you are happy with the results then rapport with your workmen is very important, as you will be allowing them into your home and may be spending a lot of time with them.

When you are discussing your project with a company you have invited to quote, think about the advice they have given you, was it useful? Have they got experience in the sort of project that you have and on the same scale? What sort of feedback have they given to your plan? How many projects do they undertake at the same time and how will they manage any overruns on projects that precede yours? How do they manage the project and communicate progress with you?

Make sure you let them know how you would like to work and see how they respond. Do they have a contract, which clearly states terms of engagement? They may operate a project management system that you can regularly access. How will they manage changes to the project specification?

Smaller companies will be able to be competitive on price but that may be a trade off with time and resource management. If one company offers to do the work at a significantly lower price that anyone else then the alarm bells should be ringing. If you have given all the companies who are going to quote, the detailed project specification, then ask them to show the cost break down in the same way, then you will have much tighter control of the budget.

Don't accept a total figure without any analysis. If they have analysed the costs for the job correctly they will have built up the final cost from all the various tasks, so giving you an analysis will not be a difficult thing to do. Of course there will be profit and contingency built in to the quote at each stage and that needs to be acknowledged after all the builder needs to make a profit, if he does not then his business will fail.

Give recognition where it is due

Once the project has been completed and if you are very happy with the work that they have carried out, then write a testimonial and recommend them to others. It is important that the good guys stay in business and are recognised.

So in summary before you finally appoint a builder (or other tradesmen) you need to make sure you have agreed the following with him and have it documented in writing covering the scope of work

- *a detailed project specification*
- *a detailed timetable showing the key stages in the project*
- *penalty clauses and/or early completion incentive*
- *agreed payment terms*

Smaller companies will be able to be competitive on price but that may be a trade off with time and resource management.

The plasterer is probably not part of the workforce.

Having your home in this state is not much fun so make sure you are prepared.

Taking control - executing your plan fairly

Does the job finish when the builder has plastered the walls and then you take over, or is he installing lights, fitted furniture and putting up curtain poles? There is the temptation to keep adding what seem like small jobs that they can do while they are still on site. But they take time and he still has to pay his workforce, so be clear about how much of the finishing tasks you expect him to do, otherwise he has every right to charge you extra at whatever rate he chooses.

Be clear about what you want

If the builder or anyone else is providing equipment, which is very common in a kitchen or bathroom, such as a shower or a dishwasher, then agree the model and specification of all the household appliances, otherwise he will purchase either the least expensive or the one he can get a good deal on. If you haven't been specific about what you want then he will make assumptions.

This also applies to areas of work where you are undecided. In this instance the builder will assume he is doing nothing and won't have built anything into his costs or his timetable. This can often be a source of many misunderstandings and problems for example if you have asked for tiles to be removed from a wall and you haven't decided if you are going to re-tile or not. The wall doesn't need re-plastering if it is to be re-tiled, but it does if it is going to be painted or wallpapered. The plasterer is probably not part of the workforce, his labour is recruited as and when he is needed and may not be available when you want him. This sort of indecision can have a significant impact on the overall project, I have seen this happen many times.

If the builder is responsible for the internal decoration of your home, make sure you supply him with all the information he needs. In my experience a builder will ask you the day before the next task is to be done exactly what you want, for instance, what colour do you want the walls to be painted because today he is going to buy the paint! If you haven't given him the information then you will probably have white or magnolia walls. Or where do you want the lights as the electrician is in today?

If you are unsure of exactly what decisions you need to make, then ask the builder to give you a checklist well in advance of any crucial stages; which you can compare with your plan and mood board. Then if there are decisions that you haven't yet made you have time to think about them before it becomes critical. Act in haste and repent at leisure.

Are you employing other trades people directly, such as the painter and decorator, electrician, carpet layer? If you are do you expect this group of people to liaise with each other or are you organising them all? It can become very complicated towards the end of an interior design project where you may have many trades on-site who are all inter dependent but do not work for each other.

It is important that you take control and ensure that all communications are shared and the project runs as smoothly as possible. This is especially so where one trade cannot proceed until another trade has completed their tasks. If they have allocated time for your project and they are then off to another job, it can be a while before they are able to return. So if you are monitoring the progress from the beginning and there is some slippage you can plan how best to resolve it.

Dealing with unforseen problems

One of the first challenges you may face is the delay in starting the project due to unforeseen problems with a previous project. This is more likely with a smaller builder who may not have the resources to cover multiple projects and it is not always a good idea for someone to start a job before finishing the previous one if they are only able to work on yours part-time.

Delays

The important thing is to keep talking and ask your builder to be realistic about any delays. If the delays are going to be significant you may want to choose somebody else to do the work, however usually the best companies are booked up ahead and may not be able to respond to you quickly. This delay will have implications further down the line with suppliers of goods and services and you may need to reschedule. The earlier everyone is aware of the possible delays then the more able they are to accommodate the change in timetable.

The important thing is to keep talking and ask your builder to be realistic about any delays.

Changes in personal and financial circumstances may well delay the start of any significant building project.

The Weather

The weather is another uncontrollable factor as there are certain things that cannot be done in either very low temperatures or in pouring rain. Most builders will build some contingency in for weather related delays, but if they are exceptional then there is nothing that can be done except be patient. Obviously you can minimise this as a problem by planning any external work at the time of the year with the best weather and the most daylight.

Materials

Materials not being delivered on time or incorrect materials being delivered can cause delays. If the materials that are to be used are very specialist, for example a particular stone from a quarry or something that is being designed and made, then delays in delivery can cause problems for the workmen who may not be able to proceed with the project without them. It is important to talk to your suppliers, make sure they understand your timetable and ask them to be realistic about their lead times. If they require large deposits, then make sure you are happy with the reliability of the company and product, and I would suggest visiting them. If you have taken responsibility for ordering the material then you are also responsible for resolving any problems that may arise. It is probably worth saying again, be clear if you are sharing the project management and who is responsible for what and that includes ordering materials.

Finances

Changes in personal and financial circumstances may well delay the start of any significant building project. Life is not always a smooth path and if something has happened that changes the family dynamics or requires your focus and energy, then I would suggest postponing any developments you had planned until you are able to review them properly. Having a lot of workmen in your home requiring your constant input and attention is stressful enough without any additional family or health stresses. Your priority must always be the people you love. If your financial circumstances have changed, then you may need to review your plans. If you have prepared a robust plan then you may be able to make adjustments that will save money without cancelling the whole project. Talk to your builder, there are always alternatives that can be considered. However if you are adding rooms, updating a kitchen or bathroom, these should be viewed as an investment in your home as they will improve its value.

Older properties

If you are making changes to an older property then the unknowns can be even more significant. Building regulations are changing and improving all the time but older properties only needed to meet the building regulations of their time and in some cases such a thing didn't exist. There are many houses that have no foundations, no damp course and the floor is laid directly on to the earth.

Any changes, extensions, refurbishments need to be carefully planned, as older properties are far more sensitive to change. Obviously if it is protected in anyway, either all of it or some of it is listed, or it is in a conservation area then there are more rigorous rules that need to be complied with. Whether it is listed or not it may be worth enlisting some professional advice about materials that may need to be used, such as lime based paints or the treatment of beams, wooden or brick floors.

Often very old properties need to be thought of as a complete project even though you may only be making changes to one part of it so that the balance in the environment isn't affected. In some properties there may be hazardous or dangerous materials discovered such as asbestos. I know of wells being discovered underground, an old thatched roof being discovered immediately under the existing roof and an inglenook fireplace behind a 1960s electric fire. An old building takes you on a journey of discovery, uncovers secrets it has held for many years, they may cause you problems, they may bring you joy but almost certainly they will surprise you.

Termites, woodworm and dry rot destroy timbers, something you do not want to find in your home.

This beautiful fireplace was covered by a 1950's tiled surround.

Listed buildings

What are listed buildings and what does it tell you about the building and how does it affect you if you are the owner?

The concept of listed buildings was introduced during World War II as a way of determining which buildings should be rebuilt if they were damaged by bombing. Shortly after the war the first list of buildings of special historical or architectural importance was compiled. In England, listed buildings are designated by the Secretary of State for Culture, Media and Sport, acting on advice from English Heritage. English Heritage assesses the building, together with any material provided to support an application, and then makes a recommendation. A very similar process exists in the rest of the UK, however it is best to check which government department is responsible for overseeing listed buildings.

The concept of listed buildings was introduced during World War II.

Interior Design Secrets . . . .

The criteria for listing a building are summarised as follows:

- *It is an interesting work of a local architect of merit or a good example of an architect of importance and influence.*

- *It forms part of an important architecturally sensitive streetscape or is part of a larger group built to a single design or purpose.*

- *It is a complete or early example of specific building type or built with a pioneering form of construction.*

- *It is a very rare survival of a specific type, which is an historically important part of an area or an industry's history.*

- *It has a definite architectural quality, or an expression of a technical or social innovation of the period, such as pumping stations and lunatic asylums.*

English Heritage assesses the building, together with any material, provided, to support an application.

A listed building does not mean that it can never be altered, demolished or developed.

This means that it is nearly impossible for what might be described as ordinary Victorian architecture, such as terraced housing, however attractive, to be listed.

The difference between Grade I and Grade II* and Grade II listing depends on the historical importance of the property. Grade I listings are buildings of exceptional national interest and 2% of all listed buildings fall into this category. Grade II* are particularly important buildings of more than special interest and account for 4% of all listed buildings and Grade II are buildings of special interest which warrant every effort being made to preserve them and account for all the remaining listed buildings. Some grants and forms of funding for renovation are not available for Grade II listed buildings. A listed building does not mean that it can never be altered, demolished or developed, but by requiring the owner to get listed building consent for the work and providing interested parties with an opportunity to comment or object, it ensures that the special historic and architectural interest of the building is taken into account in any planning decisions relating to the property

It is not true that only the facade of a listed building is protected. Listing covers all parts of the building, including the interior. Listing also protects some fixtures and fittings, as well as outbuildings, boundary walls and all other structures within the boundaries of the property. Listing protects the house as it was at the time it was added to the list, so even if you want to reinstate something that was there originally such as a fireplace, you may still need to apply for listed building planning consent. The conservation officer in your local planning office will be able to give you advice. If you want to find out if your home is listed, or if the property you are interested in purchasing is listed then go to **www.heritagegateway.org.uk** or again check with the local planning department.

Deadlines

Be wary of setting tight deadlines. Many people want the project completed before Christmas, before the baby arrives, before you move in, before exams start, and many more examples. You must be realistic about time and have a contingency plan if the deadlines aren't met. Will you need to rent the property you are in for longer? How will you cook Christmas dinner? Where will the baby sleep when it arrives? If you can avoid giving yourself fixed deadlines do. If the project overruns by a couple of weeks without clashing with a deadline then it just becomes inconvenient rather than critical. There will always be occasions when a deadline has to be met but my advice would be don't put yourself under unnecessary stress.

Procrastination!

Don't let the delays in starting your project be procrastination. It is amazing how many people accept accommodation that they don't like because they don't plan to be there for very long. In fact they don't have a plan at all and usually end up staying for much longer than they had imagined. For others they are waiting for an event to happen before they are going to take action. This could be when the children are older, when they leave home, when they have more time, or when they retire, these are all delaying tactics. If the interior of your home doesn't work for you and your family now then that is not going to change by waiting for some future event. At the very least you can explore your options and doing nothing is always an option but then it will have been an informed one.

Don't let the delays in starting your project be procrastination.

Planning your project
HOT TIPS

Remember the excitement that you felt when you first saw your home. All that enthusiasm needs to be distilled into a plan of action.

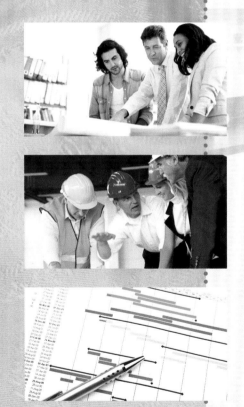

Planning is the key to keeping control of costs, time and the final design. Your action plan needs to include a floor plan, project plan and mood board and they will allow you to create a budget. These are dynamic documents that will need refining as the project gains clarity.

Carefully think about who is going to project manage what, it isn't always obvious.

Use your plan as the basis for your discussions with all the key people who are helping you achieve your interior design dream.

Choose the people you want to work with carefully. Making the right choices for you can have a major impact on how your project progresses.

Things go wrong and there will always be something unexpected that occurs. So be prepared to make decisions quickly and effectively whilst not allowing it to cause you too much stress.

3

Gathering your creative ideas together

Identifying your personal style

Ok, so now you know why you want to refurbish and you have an idea of how you are going to achieve it. But before we go any further, I would like you to use your imagination and visualise the newly created space. How does it feel when you enter the room? You want your guests to go "wow" so it goes without saying that it looks fabulous but what character are you going to give it.

I like to think of rooms or homes as falling roughly into four basic characters and from that many of the style choices are driven. Sometimes it is easier to start by thinking of our homes in terms of personality rather than try and define a style. See if you fit into one or more of the categories below.

Relaxed and familiar

The first style is relaxed and familiar. This character may appear a bit lazy and untidy, wants to be hugged and snuggle up and be informal. The style for this character would be squashy sofas, warm muted colours with lots of personal things on display. Furniture would be fairly plain and functional, a lot of lamps to create mood lighting and a mixture of hard floors with big rugs and carpets. This style would incorporate the country and rustic look that has an informal feel that appears to have been developed over a long period of time.

Smart and co-ordinated

The second style has a smarter, more co-ordinated, possibly minimalist look. This character is elegant, polite and for whom looks are important. These people may be well organised and enjoy giving a display of good taste. The style for this character would favour neat clean lines, fewer patterns and more texture, with neutral tones as a base and strong accent colours. The lighting and furniture may have a touch of glamour without being too fussy and with a preference for wooden floors with the occasional rug.

Quirky and unusual

The third style is quirky, unusual, likes to stand out from the crowd, and may even be a little wild. There won't be a particular look for this character, as they will love to mix them all up. They can be ahead of the trends. They may well have many colours and patterns with each room being completely different. The furniture and lighting will be a combination of old and new with antiques sitting alongside modern style items. Unusual collections will be on display, which are very personal and reflect a highly artistic temperament.

Smart and
co-ordinated
is elegant,
polite and
for whom
looks are
important.

Interior Design Secrets . . . .

Opulent and expensive

This fourth category is opulent, expensive and well planned, always looking at its best. These people like to be seen in all the right places and are well connected. The style for this character is formal and stately. The colours will be rich and bold from a heritage range. Furniture and lighting will be glamorous, well co-ordinated and look expensive. Fabrics will have rich textures and maybe accessorised and wooden furniture decorated with marquetry.

These are great ways to start thinking about your home and the ambience you would like to create. All this helps you further down the process when you start to choose specific colours, fabrics, lighting etc. Have fun describing the character you would like to create with your family and friends and ask them the sort of images they create.

I mentioned earlier that you should start in the rooms that have the most impact on your life, but also don't forget about your personal space where you can be alone and quiet. How this space is organised and decorated can significantly affect your mental wellbeing. All too often I see rooms, especially master bedrooms, that the homeowner hates. The satisfaction in creating a space that you love to be in can't be underestimated, so don't forget those special 'me' spaces.

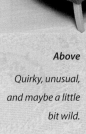

Above

Quirky, unusual, and maybe a little bit wild.

Start gathering ideas for a mood board

It is great imagining how your home could look. Later in this chapter we will look specifically at the advantages of creating a mood board. When do you need to start creating one? I think it is something you should be thinking of right from the beginning of the design process. Indeed the inspiration for redesigning your home, may have come from something you saw that you loved in a magazine, or you saw at a hotel. It helps you establish the "general room feel" rather than a specific "must have" item. This should be the first item on your mood board. This gives life and form to all those thoughts of what it is you would like to achieve with your design.

Your mood board should reflect what you see when you close your eyes. This is why you are embarking on this project, to give yourself your dream home.

Your mood board should reflect what you see when you close your eyes.

Your own happy memories

The inspiration for your scheme may have come from a holiday photo, a piece of old fabric, a flower, anything that sets off your imagination and creates your inspiration. These are the things that will go on your mood board. Remember that this board is for your personal use and doesn't need to follow any particular format, it may be covered in Post-It Notes, scribbles or strange objects, and that doesn't matter. It is purely a means to an end and the end is a fabulous home.

Holiday photographs can be the inspiration for colours, shapes and patterns.

Your neighbours

If you have recently moved into your property and looking for inspiration, a good place to start could be with your neighbours' homes. This is especially relevant if you have an older property. Their homes may still have some of the original features that have been removed from yours, for example fireplaces, coving, ceiling roses and other internal architecture that at different times have been unfashionable and often removed. They may have changed the configuration of their rooms, extended or enhanced the space in such a way that would suit you. Basically don't re-invent the wheel. Benefit from other people's experiences and then make their ideas your own by giving them your personality.

Stately Homes can be a great source of inspiration and ideas.

Stately homes!

If you love traditional elegance then make a visit to you local stately home. There are some minor stately homes that aren't as grand as somewhere like Blenheim Palace or Chatsworth House, but these can give you some information about colours, styles of textiles and furniture that once was fashionable. You can see how they would have dressed the windows, displayed pictures and mirrors and set the layout of the rooms.

Your home as it used to be

If you have an older property it is great fun to find out more about who once lived there. How they lived and the interior design style they may have adopted. This is now easy on the Internet where

you can look through the censuses and find out names, occupations and numbers of people living there and bring the story of your home to life. There may even be some old photographs in the archives for you to access. Different eras have had distinctive styles which may give you inspiration, for example the Victorian era, the Arts and Crafts style, the Art Deco period are all very different in colours, textures, patterns and shapes. It will certainly make you feel part of your home's continuing story and that you in turn will pass the legacy on to someone else. In Chapter 4 we will talk further about styling older properties.

Interior design magazines

The very best place to start is with interior design magazines. There are a large variety out there, specialising in different style properties and featuring different rooms, especially kitchens and bathrooms. Many of the magazines give you the opportunity to buy back copies so if they have run articles that you are particularly interested in you can order them.

The beauty of magazines is you can cut out pages that contain any looks that particularly interest you and you can write on them why you especially liked specific things for future reference. It may be a mirror on one page, the lighting on another and the flooring elsewhere. They can be cut out and saved and put on your mood board alongside your choice of wall colours and fabrics.

A word of caution, don't get too carried away with the 'current look'. Remember you are creating a design for you that will still look fabulous in a few years' time and not become dated, so pick out those single elements that take your breath away. This is why I strongly advise anyone not to copy an interior design in its entirety, it needs to reflect your personality and your home's character. You may have always wanted a chandelier, an aquarium or full-length silk curtains. They may be rejected later but if you don't include them now they will never have the opportunity to be part of your home.

Interior design company websites

The Internet is another obvious starting point, although anything you print out from it will only be as good as the quality of the pictures on the website and your printer. However it is great for ideas from around the world. It is a good place to access many suppliers, review their product range and prices before walking down

The very best place to start is with interior design magazines.

the High Street. You can order brochures which can also give you inspiration, for example, of how to use a fabric as they often show their products together.

Maybe there is a chair in front of a curtain with a cushion using all their fabrics. Soft furnishing companies will design collections of fabrics to be used together. The danger of only using one supplier is the look created can appear over coordinated and lack individuality. So use them to help you with ideas but not to dictate the final design.

Exhibitions on homes and living

There are many exhibitions on homes and living that give you an opportunity to see and touch something different. They will almost always offer special discounts, but remember only make a purchase if it fits in with your plan and mood board. The best plan may be to avoid making a purchase until your mood board is completed.

Favourite things you already have

In Chapter 4 we look at choosing what you have already that is suitable and appropriate, or indeed much loved.

Most likely you won't be replacing everything you own, so a printed out photo of your chosen favourites will probably be among the first on the mood board. In older properties you may have period features such as a fireplace or perhaps some stained glass, which could well be a vital focal point. These will need to appear on the mood board.

In Chapter 8 we look at a whole range of creative ideas for treating windows, floors, walls and putting together those finishing touches in a way that reflects you, and the style of your property.

Choosing fabrics can be a daunting task if you are not sure what you are looking for.

You may have a favourite leather chair or you have some fabric that you want to use.

Start a collection of samples

Order samples from as many suppliers as you are interested in. There are three types of samples.

A normal sample will be a relatively small piece of fabric or wallpaper, which will give you the general colour, texture and pattern. These are ideal for your mood board and most suppliers are happy to send them out.

There are the large returnable samples, which allow you to see a full pattern repeat and get a better feel for the overall look. You would only want to order these when you have almost decided on your chosen fabric and wallpaper and you want to be sure. These samples normally have to be returned within a month or there is a charge.

The third type of sample is a cutting. This is a sample of fabric from the roll of fabric that you are purchasing. In the case of natural fabrics such as silk there can be colour variations between rolls of fabrics, so if you need to check for exactly the right colour, you may want to order a cutting before finally ordering. It is also possible to order sample flooring, wood finishes, and metal finishes for lighting or curtain poles.

It is very important that you request samples of all the fabrics, carpets and wood finishes that you wish to consider so that not only can you see how they look together, but you can also see them in your light.

Light can significantly change colour tones, depending on the amount of light in the room and the direction in which the room is facing. Electric light also has an impact so you need to make sure that your mood board looks great in the day and at night.

All suppliers offer a sample service and are very happy to send to you any fabrics you request. This is very important if you are researching on the internet where the true colour, pattern, scale and proportion can be very difficult to see. When you are requesting samples ask about stock levels, and delivery times and cost. Many suppliers carry minimal stock and if what you want needs to be made and shipped from the other side of the world it can take months before it is available. This may have a bearing on your choice especially if you have set yourself a deadline in which to complete your project.

The more information you gather the better decisions you will make. Once you start to display all these items together you may find that a look and feel emerges that you hadn't expected and create something far more stylish than you have ever done before.

Create your mood board

Professional interior designers use mood boards both for commercial customers and for private clients to clearly explain their concepts and ideas they have for the space; which they have been commissioned to redesign. It forms the basis of the proposal and design costs. So why not take advantage of a well used and respected process that the interior design industry regularly use.

A mood board is simply a place where pictures and samples of everything you are considering putting together can be gathered, viewed, considered and discussed. It doesn't need to a big hard board, it can be a file or a box where everything is collated.

There is no right or wrong way in how to produce a mood board. You will be amazed how adventurous you may become as you can test colours and patterns together you would not have ordinarily considered without any financial commitment. This should be fun and exciting, allowing your creative juices to flow, it does not need to be a professionally put together ideas board this is for yours and your family's eyes only. Have fun.

The sort of things to include would be:

- *paint and fabric swatches*
- *pictures of proposed furniture and lighting*
- *examples of the colour of the wood*
- *pictures of window treatments*
- *trimmings and carpet samples*
- *pictures of tile examples*
- *technical drawings of kitchens, bathrooms and floor plans*
- *room settings that have inspired your design*

Inspiration may come from a figure in history and by including them on your moodboard means you don't lose the initial rationale.

Creating a moodboard allows you to share your ideas clearly with the rest of your family.

Gathering all your ideas together in one place makes it a lot easier to see how your proposed scheme will work.

When you have collected all your samples and photos it is a matter of laying them on a large board together. At this point the items don't have to be in any particular order they just need to be viewed together so you can see what works and what doesn't.

I recommend using an A2 board so that you have plenty of room to display everything in one place. You may want to have a board per room. This allows you to not only look at each design individually but also see how they fit together as a whole.

You want to be able to attach and detach the samples and pictures from the board as the look develops. A magnet board with magnets works well, otherwise something that can accommodate mapping pins, double sided tape or spray mount.

The process of planning also allows other members of the family to have an input, you can share your vision with; which is very difficult to do verbally, and makes re-designing your home a collaborative affair and avoids all those misunderstandings. If others are contributing to your design you can give them their own board to create. And then compare and contrast ideas, selecting the best from each to create a whole new mood board.

Once you start to put your ideas together it is always surprising how something you thought would be perfect very quickly looks out of place. It may mean that the item that you would like needs to be a different size or in a different colour. It may be that it doesn't fit in with the overall personality of the design, maybe too glitzy, too quirky or just too boring.

As you build up your bank of samples, including paint colours, you can start not only to see how the various colours work but also the textures and patterns which are equally as important and give any design depth and interest.

Where you have existing items that you want to use in the new scheme, take photographs of them so that they can be included. Then when you are choosing a fabric for the curtains for instance, you can lay the photo alongside all your other choices and see if it works with your design or not

If it isn't quite right try and be objective about why you feel like that and if you are finding that difficult, recruit some help. Go back to basics and imagine the look and feel you would like given yours and the property's personality. Your design is probably missing some key element or one of your choices does not have integrity within the design. You are most creative when you are not under stress or pressure, so if you have given yourself plenty of time, the solution will come to you.

Live with the mood board for a while. Sometimes you need to see it afresh before you can properly review it. If you have ever painted a picture, often you need to walk away from it and then return to see where it needs to be improved. A mood board needs to be looked at in the same way, after all you are creating a picture of your design.

Keep the mood board in the room for which it has been created. This will give you a better feel of the final effect. Look at it in daylight and at night and take notice of how you feel about it. If you love it, then you know you have created the best scheme for your home. Then when the project has been completed, compare it to your mood board. In my experience, whilst the mood board has produced a fantastic design, the final outcome is usually even better. You cannot beat seeing all your ideas finally take shape. It will inspire you to never take on another interior design without producing a mood board first.

Keep the mood board in the room for which it has been created.

Gathering your creative ideas together

51

The benefits of making a mood board

- A mood board collates all your ideas so you can see how they will work together.
- A mood board can encourage you to be more adventurous in your choices. A scheme can be well planned but lack that 'wow' factor.
- A mood board allows you to explore interesting and unusual ideas.
- On a mood board you can consider many alternatives before making your final choices.
- A mood board gives you the opportunity to explore your thoughts with others.
- If you need to re-think something then on a mood board you can assess how it will impact your design.
- Once you have finally finished your mood board then you can start establishing all the costs.

A mood board allows you to explore interesting and unusual ideas.

*Gathering all your ideas together in one place makes it a
lot easier to see how your proposed scheme will work.*

HOT TIPS

*Identifying your personal style helps you to narrow down your
choices. There is such a wide range of choice for anything to do
with the home that you need to establish a selection criteria
from which to start.*

*Inspiration and ideas can come from anywhere, it maybe from
publications, the Internet, places you have stayed or even your
neighbour's home. The history of your home may also help you
establish a style and look.*

*Collect samples of everything you wish to consider for your
interior design scheme. You need to see the true colour, texture
and pattern as well as looking at them in the light of your home.*

*Collate all your ideas on a mood board and have fun doing it. This
will help you stay focused and motivated through the uncertain
decision making stages.*

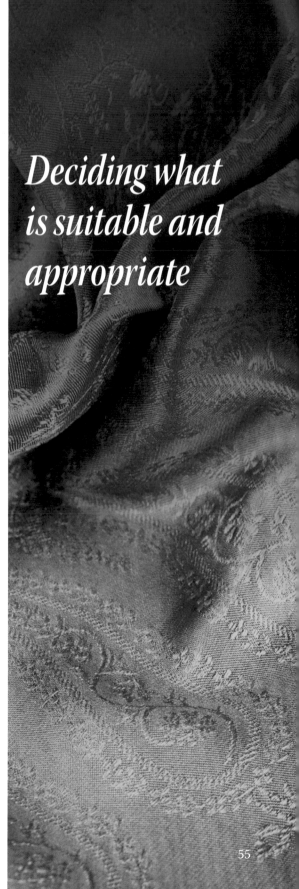

4

Deciding what is suitable and appropriate

We've looked at how you will plan your project, and how you can start gathering ideas together, but there is one very important consideration that will underpin your design plan: that is what is appropriate and suitable for the age and character of your house. This will then help you determine which of the things that you have already can stay and what is no longer appropriate or useful and should go.

The character of older properties

All properties should have a feel and vibe that your interior design needs to connect with. Most people would agree that a white minimalist look would not look right in a beamed thatched cottage, but then again somebody who likes a modern minimalist style wouldn't be attracted to buying a beamed thatched cottage. So your design and character needs to be generally congruent with the style of the property. Chapter 8 will give you lots of tips and ideas for adding personal and appropriate character to your design scheme.

Restoration of an old property needs to be sympathetic but that doesn't mean it has to be an historic replica.

Although it is great to show the varying interior design styles that your home has lived through, be selective about what you choose to keep and what needs to go. You may have inherited some monstrosities such as an old linoleum floor, 1960s large spotlights, pine clad walls or a brick effect chimney breast. If they are not appropriate to the look and feel of your design (or the period of your property) then change them. Tastes change over time and your home will evolve with them just as it has up to now. If you are unsure of how the interior architecture in particular would have looked, ask to look inside a neighbour's house. They may have retained more of the original features and give you some ideas.

Not everything that was originally there needs to be put back and certainly not if it isn't in keeping with your design, but you may want to use elements of it. For instance, the style of coving, the type of doors, decorative stained glass in the windows, or the tiles on the floor are all features that you may wish to reintroduce. Of course don't be afraid to add some modern touches too, not just the technological ones. We'll look at how to blend these in sympathetically later in this chapter. If you are extending your home in any way, the extension may well be a very modern part of your home and your design must integrate it with the rest of the property. You may have a home that has been extended many times over many years so your design will need to bring all those stages together and still create a stylishly modern home.

An evolving entity – blending old and new styles

Restoration of an old property needs to be sympathetic but that doesn't mean it has to be an historic replica. It can often be more difficult to create an interior design for an older property. There may be structural limitations. It might be listed or parts of it listed. Special materials may need to be used and accommodating modern plumbing and wiring may well be a challenge. Of course it can make things more exciting as you develop a plan to overcome any difficulties. Who knows what you may discover? You may live in a house that has changed shape and style many times over its lifetime and therefore doesn't belong to any one particular era.

All these factors need to be taken into account in your design but you are not living in a museum and therefore it still has to work for you both functionally and visually. There is so much information out there that can show you how something would

The original window
latches (below) were
the inspiration for the
pole and finials for
the curtains (left).

have looked in a particular time period and you may want to use it as an inspiration
for you to develop your ideas. In nearly all areas of interior design there are heritage
ranges and companies who specialise in this field. In fact if you go back in time most
people would have lived with a combination of styles from different eras, some
being inherited, some home-made and some bought. It wasn't until the Industrial
Revolution and the ability to mass-produce anything that the modern man has been
able to buy most of what he wants from new. So try to think of your house as an
evolving entity and not stuck in a time warp. One day you will pass on your home to
someone else who will in turn make their mark and thus continue its evolution.

One of the challenges with an older property is that many of the rooms we use
now simply didn't exist when the house was originally built. This is certainly true of
the bathroom, which is a very modern feature. However it is possible to create an
elegant timeless feel, by carefully selecting the appropriate look. This may be with
the style of tiles, or a combination of tongue and groove and tiles to create a more
country look. There are a number of heritage style sanitary ware ranges to choose
from. The standalone bath is an obvious choice recreating the look from the more
wealthy homes where they would have been filled manually. You can choose old

*Try to think
of your house
as an evolving
entity and not
stuck in a
time warp.*

style light and bathroom fittings and maybe shutters at the window. You will not be able to faithfully reproduce an old bathroom so it is more about creating the right atmosphere.

The kitchen is another room that has changed beyond recognition and you wouldn't want to give up modern conveniences just to create a certain look. The style of the kitchen chosen can help create a heritage look. The design of the doors, hinges and handles all contribute to the traditional style. Think about having some stand alone pieces of furniture so that the kitchen looks like it has been put together over time and avoid a fitted kitchen look. Perhaps you can vary the types of finishes, for example a combination of painted and natural wood. An Aga certainly gives an older home more of a country kitchen feel that goes so well in quaint cottages. Having an Aga does change the way you cook and it is an expensive item, so think about it carefully before making an investment.

If you live in an old workers cottage it may not even have had an internal staircase just a ladder. With this sort of refurbishment you should aim to reflect the overall style and feel you want to create rather than trying to reproduce something from that era. This is the same with doors and windows. It may be the door handles or the window catches that have an old worldly feel that you can include in order to create the right look. This is the same with coving, architraves and other architectural features, they do not have to be exact replicas of a bygone age but there are plenty of designs available that have a classic older style. You can visit reclamation yards which depending on their stock can have an amazing selection of unusual objects that might suit the age of your home. If you don't want anything to look too new, you want it to have a few knocks and scuffs, then this would be a good place to start. There are also auction houses that specialise in house clearances and you may find what you want at a very good price.

As mentioned before you are not producing a house in a time warp as the stately homes try to. In being sympathetic to your home's history and by doing a little research you may be inspired to adopt a particular style and apply it to a more modern use. For example if you have a study or playroom this would have only been accessible to the very rich, so again think about the overall general style rather

An Aga certainly gives an older home more of a country kitchen feel that goes so well in quaint cottages.

Interior Design Secrets . . . .

Left:
There are some features that are a gift to any character property interior design scheme.

Below:
This was a new pine door leading to an extension. A makeover inspired by the glazed front door bridged the old part of the house with the new.

than trying to copy a room from another era. There is a museum in London called the Geffrye Museum, which is devoted to the history of the home, and gives an insight into how domestic interiors in England have evolved. There are room sets for every era including one from each decade of the twentieth century when the changes to our lifestyle were most rapid. It is very interesting and well worth a visit, it will put you in touch with the style and feel of an era so you can adapt the ideas for modern purposes.

Blending in modern technology and comfort

Some of the beautiful old cottages that some fortunate people have the pleasure to live in are probably on a different socio-economic scale to those who first lived there and many of our everyday household necessities would never have existed even for the very wealthy. Electricity is one of the things that has revolutionised our lives. We no longer have to work and sleep according to the daylight hours, we can have instant power at the flick of a switch and we can have light, sound, pictures, communication and many other modern day amenities, but they don't always look very attractive. Careful thought may need to be given as to how to blend them in sympathetically. Lighting is an obvious important factor in any interior design, both in how the room is to be lit and the type of light fittings you choose. We'll look further at lighting in Chapter 6.

There are ranges of products that can give a traditional feel to a modern room.

Deciding what is suitable and appropriate

Slimline televisions no longer need to be housed in large cumbersome pieces of furniture.

Televisions

Television is a large part of most family's lives and is now a prominent feature in the main living space. How does your television currently work in your living room? Is it the first thing you see when you walk in? Slimline televisions no longer need to be housed in large cumbersome pieces of furniture but still need allocated space as well as power points and any other connections for them to work. They often need to be connected to satellite boxes, DVD players etc. They are an interior designer's nightmare and often any pictures you will see in magazines don't include any of this equipment for that reason. But they are a part of our modern world so don't ignore them but incorporate them into your design.

All televisions now have an internet point so if you ensure you have one where you plan to place your television you will be able to access TV on demand. If you have an intelligent sound system you will be able to play music in a room chosen via your smartphone and lights, blinds and curtains can be turned on or off at your request whether you are there or not. Trailing cables and wires can destroy the balance and design of a room, so if you can plan to have them hidden from view or completely eliminated that can only be a good thing. There are many companies out there that can give you advice and create a design.

Interior Design Secrets . . . .

There are ways of making televisions look less obvious. They can be mounted on a wall and look like a picture, remember you need to plan the wiring carefully to avoid unsightly trailing wires. I have seen a television mounted on a smoked glass background and visually it almost disappeared. Of course a television can be part of a piece of furniture and now that they are narrower this is easier than ever before. It may be that the furniture frames the television or it is discretely placed on a shelf that can be pulled out when needed. It is hard not to have the television as the main feature as not only is it a normally large black square but all the furniture usually faces it as well. Another way to make a television visually less imposing is to introduce black accents elsewhere in the room. You could introduce some table lamps with black shades, black cushions, pictures with dark frames, a rug with a black or dark pattern. This then creates balance in the room and stops the eye only being drawn to the big black box in the corner.

When you are planning your interior design don't ignore these things, they need to be integrated in to your scheme otherwise potentially they could ruin the overall effect. The same goes for stereo systems, computers, printers, game consoles and any other technical equipment that is regularly used and will be on display. They are part of our modern world and our homes need to work for our current life styles not those of our ancestors.

Televisions can be mounted on a wall and look like a picture, remember you need to plan the wiring carefully to avoid unsightly trailing wires.

If you are keeping the radiators, then think about their positions.

Radiators are now available in a range of styles including a classic style like this one.

Radiators

Radiators are another modern feature which must be included in any design. The average radiator is not an attractive thing and certainly would not have been part of an older property. However, I don't think anyone wants to give up central heating for aesthetic reasons. So if you want to keep those radiators, what can you do? One of the options is to have radiator covers, which come in many styles and finishes and can be co-ordinated with your other furniture, or they can be painted the same colour as the wall, so that they become visually less obtrusive or choose a style of radiator that looks authentic. There are radiator designs with Victorian decoration, which are chunky with pretty designs and can be very attractive. They can often be seen in old civic buildings and is the sort of object that can be bought at a reclamation centre. They would certainly suit the style of property built around the beginning of the twentieth century. There are some very modern radiator designs in an array of colours that are more like pieces of art and which can be a feature, for instance in a bathroom.

If you are doing quite a major refurbishment then you may have the opportunity to install underfloor heating, which is far more energy efficient, and removes the problem of radiators altogether. Underfloor heating restricts your choice of flooring, but if that isn't an issue then it should be considered. Underfloor heating can run on gas or electricity and is cheap and easy to install.

If you are keeping the radiators, then think about their positions. It has been usual practice to put them below windows, but with double-glazing and better insulated houses this is no longer necessary. If you would like to have floor length curtains, you don't want the heat to be trapped behind them so don't leave the radiator there. Also be careful not to place the radiator on a wall where logically another piece of furniture will go.

If your radiators are not in the right place then it is a relatively simple job for a plumber to move them, you don't want your design being compromised by having radiators in the wrong place. Finally if you are planning to add radiators you need to check that your boiler can cope with the additional load. A registered plumber should be able to help and advise you on these matters.

Double glazing

Double glazing has already been mentioned and can be a key component in energy saving throughout the house. Heat loss through single glazed windows can be reduced up to 50% by introducing double glazing. The double glazing industry has come a long way since the first mass market windows of the 1970s and 80s and they are now able to copy almost any style of window. They are very easy and quick to install, generally there is very little damage done to window and door openings if this is a worry for you. You may have beautiful stained glass or leaded windows that you would like to keep or if your house is listed you may need to seek permission if you would like to install double glazing. If you want to keep your old windows but they are drafty, then thick, heavy curtains with interlining can act as good insulation. These are all factors that need to be considered when you are putting your mood board and plan together.

Carpets and flooring

Fitted carpets are another modern phenomena. Whilst carpets and rugs have been around for a long time they certainly haven't always been on the floor. There was a time when carpets were far too expensive to be walked on and in the days before synthetic fibres very difficult to keep clean. They would have adorned walls in the same way as tapestries or even as a covering for a table. Only the very wealthy had the comfort of something soft to walk on.

There has recently been a move away from the fitted carpet in preference to a hard floor with a rug. This combination can suit any style and age of property, as there is a fantastic choice of hard floors both from natural and synthetic materials and an amazing selection of rugs. Rugs can be specifically designed for you or some companies have a range of patterns for which you can choose your own colours. Traditional hard floors can be expensive and may not be practical if you need to think about sound proofing or your floors are so uneven that without major changes a hard floor wouldn't lay on top.

> *There has recently been a move away from the fitted carpet in preference to a hard floor with a rug.*

*The rug is the focal point for the seating arrangement
and breaks up a dominating wooden floor.*

You may also prefer a fitted carpet for warmth and comfort, especially in the bedrooms. The next thing to consider is where is the carpet to be used. Is it be fitted in a busy traffic area such as the hallway or in an area less vulnerable to dirty outdoor shoes such as a bedroom. Generally the more patterned a carpet is the less likely it is to show up the marks and a mix of natural and synthetic fibres are recommended to give it durability and beauty. There is an enormous range of prices and quality, so always check the suitability of the carpet. Most carpets are labelled giving recommendations of where they can be used. The choice of colour and pattern of carpet depends on the effect you would like to achieve as well as how it might blend in with the period feel of your room. For example, do you want the carpet to be a beautiful design and therefore the focal point of the space on the main stairs? Or do you want it as a backdrop to interesting pieces of furniture or a beautifully dressed bed? Your mood board will help you see how your proposed carpet or alternative hard flooring harmonises with the rest of the scheme and the period look. In Chapter 8 we look further at different types of flooring.

What stays and what goes

This is a very important question and should be consciously considered in your design. Whatever is staying may have an enormous impact on your interior design scheme; its feeling and look maybe very influential such as a fireplace or wooden beams. I had a client who had an original seventeenth century brick flooring which was not only beautiful but also a very strong visual feature and that was our starting point for the colour scheme of that room. If this is true for you then it must be on your mood board, it can't be ignored otherwise you are missing an important element of the final design.

If something is going but being directly replaced with an updated version, then always take the opportunity to review your practical needs. For example do you still need to seat the same number of people regularly? Can a pouf replace a chair for the odd occasion when you need to sit an extra person? It is very easy to become so familiar with our surroundings that we don't often question what we really need. When a room or house is being refurbished, that is the ideal time to ask yourself what do you need and why.

Moving things around

Of course not replacing everything is a way of saving money and time. You may have recently replaced an expensive item or you may feel that what you have is perfectly fine and you are reluctant to replace it. There are always opportunities to move older items into other rooms rather than purely replace them. Older chairs may go into bedrooms, lamps into the study, this then gives you the opportunity to start afresh in the room you are decorating. There are many reasons why you might not want to buy new things everywhere, but whatever you keep, must still fit in with the overall design.

Whatever is staying may have an enormous impact on your interior design scheme.

This old nursing chair was recovered to create a pretty co-ordinating bedroom chair.

> *Ensure that everything that remains in the room is included as part of the design.*

Everything has its place and purpose

Do not be tempted to ignore something because you will be replacing it at some time in the future. Life does not always quite go according to plan it may be something you mean to do but never get around to. This is especially true when having spent a lot of time and effort in re-furbishing your home, the enthusiasm wanes a little and you just want to complete the project. So if it is not being replaced as part of the refurbishment then include it in your scheme and mood board. If it is something you really don't like then please replace it otherwise it will compromise your design and annoy you forever.

Of course there are some things you would not want to alter once the work has been completed, for example lighting or moving things like radiators. So ensure that everything that remains in the room is included as part of the design and doesn't look as if it has been forgotten.

If something is to remain but it is not in as good a condition as you would like, then can it be enhanced? For example a wooden floor can be revarnished, cracked coving can be repaired and adding a ceiling rose could really make a difference, stripping old doors and renewing handles will not only change the way the object looks but also bring an individuality to your design you had probably never thought of.

Have a good clear out

It is a truism in our modern society that we have too much 'stuff'. Redecorating a room is an ideal time to have a serious sort out. This always takes a lot longer than you would have thought as it is constantly amazing how much a relatively small cupboard can hold, let alone a wardrobe or indeed an attic. So allocate enough time and don't leave it until the night before the decorator or builder is due to arrive to sort things out. The danger is it will just end up being hidden again.

William Morris, a famous interior designer in the Arts and Crafts movement and innovator in design methods and techniques, famously said 'you should only have in your home that which is useful or beautiful'. If you apply that rule to everything you have, it soon becomes apparent what needs to go.

Another good benchmark is if you haven't used something or worn something for a year then you are probably not going to need it again. Unless you can see a way of creatively revamping it to fit in with your design scheme, you certainly wouldn't miss it if it weren't there. The opportunity to recycle has never been easier. You can sell on eBay or at car boot sales. You can give them away to other members of the family, charity shops, church or a local hospital. There are various charities that will pick up items of furniture and give them to someone who needs them. This is much better than just taking something to the tip. It is a good habit to think about getting rid of something each time you buy something new. This will stop you filling all the space you have just created by having a clear out.

There are alternative ways of storing things, especially "information", for instance can all those paper files and photo albums be stored electronically? It is a great feeling when you have had a good sort out. It can be quite cathartic, a feeling of clearing out the old to make way for the new, which can be very significant if this coincides with a change in your life's circumstances. This will also give you an opportunity to assess your true storage needs and may save you some money. The more cupboards you have the more you are likely to fill them. Be disciplined even if you are a natural hoarder

Treasured objects

There is a special category of items that you will want to keep, but you are not always sure what to do with them, and that is your "treasured objects". This category may be special because these things remind you of the person who gave it to you, or of a special place and time in your life. It may be a hand-made gift from a child or friend. Whatever your treasured objects are, if they are important to you then they should be included in your design. They can be displayed together to create an impact for example a group of family photos or a display of objects that you collect or are passionate about.

I had a client who had so many shoes that rather than try and create cupboard space for them we decided to line a wall with shelves where all her shoes could both be stored and displayed. If you have a number of different items can you create an eclectic collection by displaying them together in a cabinet or shelf ? Everyone loves to look at unusual objects and they can be a great talking point for guests. You may even decide to make them the focal point of the room. If it is a growing collection you will need to think how you will accommodate that and if it is valuable, how you make it secure whilst still enjoying it. If you have a collection of items that you are struggling to house then now is the time to look dispassionately

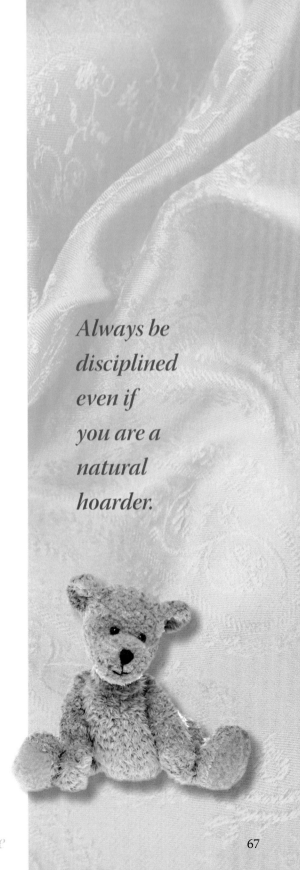

Always be disciplined even if you are a natural hoarder.

This gorgeous early Victorian fireplace was bought from an architectural salvage yard.

at it and decide what should stay and what should go. If you find that too hard to do by yourself then ask for help from family or friends. Maybe you can keep a representative sample of the collection or perhaps it is time to move on and pass it on to someone else who can continue to enjoy it.

It is always suggested that when you are having a wardrobe clear-out, do it with a friend who you know will be honest. The same can be said about all those items in your home that you have lived with for years and no longer see. Another pair of fresh eyes can often give some very valuable advice. Always ask yourself why do you want to keep it. If you can't think of anything then it is probably time for that article to go. Celebrate the fact you have finally sorted out that part of your life and remember that often "less is more".

Finding creative alternatives

Clearing out and designing your home is an opportunity for a new start rather than just redecorating and replacing furniture. It can be very difficult to let go or change, but that shouldn't be a reason on its own not to do it. Nothing is impossible; there is always a solution to every problem. Even if the solution may prove too expensive or too disruptive for you at this time, but at least you will have explored all the possibilities.

The Internet is a great resource for exploring different alternatives or solutions to a problem. There will almost certainly be someone who has done something similar to what you would like to do and will be willing to give advice. You can even type into a search engine your question it can be as simple as "can I build a fireplace out of railway sleepers?" or as complicated as "how do I build a balustrade?" and you will be amazed at the response you will get. If the answers you receive aren't quite right then you may need to refine the question to (for example) "is it safe to build a fireplace out of railway sleepers?" or "who can design and build a balustrade?" The power of the Internet has allowed specialist manufacturers to bring their products to a mass market and allows you to find them without even leaving your home. So don't let the high street be the limit of your shopping experience, whilst there is no substitute for seeing and touching material, there is only so much a shop can stock and certainly they cannot offer a complete bespoke service.

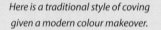
Here is a traditional style of coving given a modern colour makeover.

Placing antique furniture in a modern room can look fabulous.

The character of the property needs to be reflected in the interior design scheme but you shouldn't try to recreate an historic replica.

Many properties are a blend of different interior styles so remember to think of your house as a complete home and choose carefully the features you want to keep, lose or re-introduce.

No one wants to live in a museum so blending modern technology into an older property can be a challenge but not impossible. With some planning and consultation you can ensure that you do not have to compromise your design scheme for the latest gismo!

How much do we keep and how much should go? By planning your interior design scheme this decision becomes a lot easier. Most of us have too much 'stuff', so take the opportunity to declutter when you redecorate.

If you are having problems in imagining what your property may have looked like in the past, start by looking at your neighbour's home - they may still have the very feature that your home lacks.

5

Understanding colour, pattern and fabrics

The red walls of this dining room work perfectly in a room used for entertaining and lively conversation and complement the strong colours of the furniture and fabrics.

Colour is such an important part of our world, it can change a mood, it can change the scale and proportion of things, and it is probably one element that everyone has a strong opinion on. At the very least you will know what colours you don't like. We use colour in everyday language to describe our state of health, the weather, feelings; they represent seasons, celebrations and even our sex.

Using colour, pattern and fabrics is the fun part of interior design and yet many people are afraid of getting it wrong. On a mood board you can see how they work without taking any risks and you may decide to be adventurous and play around with a range of options. We'll have a look at the important things to bear in mind so that you can feel confident about making wise and stylish choices.

Using colour effectively

Everything you purchase comes in a colour and therefore it is an important element of every purchase decision.

In this section we are referring to colour as appearing on walls, flooring, fabrics, woodwork and other surfaces.

- **Combining colours** - *the colour wheel can be used as a guideline of how to combine colours if you don't know where to start, or it may suggest some alternative combinations that you previously wouldn't have thought of. How you combine colours can be a very personal choice and if you are confident with colour you probably don't need to worry, but for most people a fear of getting it wrong often leads to a an interior design scheme that lacks that 'wow' factor.*

- **Types of colour** *– tints, hues and shades. This can be very confusing and they all have a slightly different meaning but for the purposes of decorating your home it refers to the intensity of the colour.*

    *A **tint** is a colour to which white has been added to make it lighter. A tint is always lighter than the original colour.*

    *A **hue** is a colour in a pure state on the light spectrum*

    *A **shade** is a colour to which black or some other dark colour has been added therefore a shade is always darker than the original colour.*

    Shade also explains a slight degree of difference between colours.

    All tints and shades are considered to be tones and are softer than the original colour.

How you combine colours can be a very personal choice.

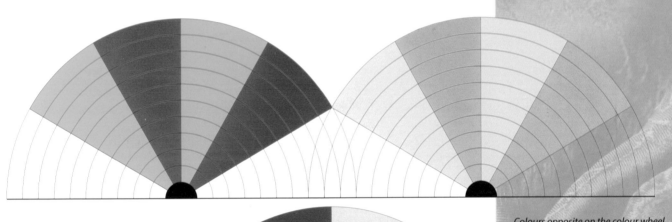

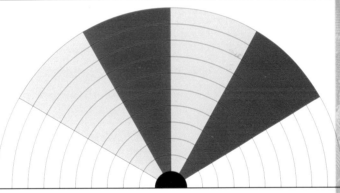

Colours opposite on the colour wheel will always compliment each other but they need to also have the same depth of colour.

The bold red changes the pale green to almost grey.

The more colours you introduce to your scheme, the more important it is to use the same tone.

A bold rich colour will dominate too much if all the other colours in the design scheme are pale and delicate. In fact the bold colour can leach the colour out of anything around it that lacks its power.

The greater the number of different colours you are going to introduce the more important it is that they have the same intensity, so whilst colours opposite on the colour wheel look great together and are often a very bold combination, colours that are on the same circumference of the colour wheel can also look great and create a harmonious look. These are colours with the same degree of tint or shade.

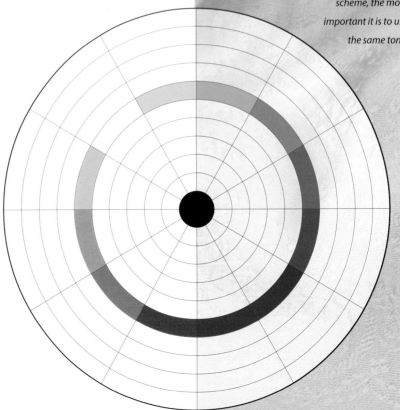

Swatches of fabric will help you choose the right tone of colour when you are building up your colour scheme.

When selecting paint colours it is often worthwhile looking at a variety of shades around the initial choice. When colours are used together they can affect each other's appearance. This is especially so with off-whites where the appearance of the colour can change quite dramatically when it is viewed alongside another stronger colour. For example, the cream you liked may now look slightly green, or the light grey now looks blue. Different types of light will also affect the colour. Is your room facing north with a cool natural light or south with a warm natural light? How does your artificial lighting affect the colour? Only by looking at the colour in your own environment will you know if it is right for that location or not; which is why it is important to collect samples The proportions in which you are using colour should also be reflected on the mood board so its full impact can be assessed. Be careful about trying to remember colours, carrying colours in your head is more difficult than you imagine, so always get a sample. Don't rely on someone else's description of a colour either. I once had a client that having said he liked the colour peach I discovered he meant terracotta!

- *Proportions of colour are an important consideration in your interior design scheme and ideally on your mood board you are able to see how those proportions work. If you are planning to have a neutral colour palette with an accent of red for example in a lamp shade or cushions, then the mood board needs to show the colours in roughly the same proportions as your proposed design. In most rooms, the wall and floor coverings are the largest elements within the scheme and therefore the colour, pattern and texture of these should also dominate your mood board providing a backdrop for the lighting, furniture and fabrics that you are planning to use. By doing this you will be able to judge whether you have enough or too great a variety of colours.*

- *If you are frightened of using colour or making an expensive mistake, but want to be more adventurous, then I suggest using a bright bold colour as an accent rather than as a main colour. The base colour can be neutral tones, such as creams and greys, which will complement any bright accent colour beautifully. The accent colour can be on the cushions, tie backs, lamp shades, rug, towels in a bathroom, bed throw in a bedroom almost anything that is not so big to be over powering but not too small so that it goes unnoticed. Also, the accent colour needs to appear in more than one place so that it looks part of the interior design scheme and not an accidental addition. Accent colours can be changed easily. So if you are someone who becomes bored with the look of a room quickly, then this is an easy and effective way to bring in the changes*

- *Colour and the effect it has on space and its proportions may be an important factor in your home. Generally anything that is dark will advance and look bigger when alongside anything light and the converse for anything that is light in colour. In this way you can change the visual proportions of a room.*

An accent colour can be as subtle as a covered button.

The striking red accents in the lamp shades and curtains was a leap of faith for this young couple's bedroom, but it really brings the whole room to life.

Stunning Osborne & Little wallpaper is the colourful 'wow' factor in this bedroom.

Small amounts of colour can really have an impact as seen here with Tom Faulkner furniture.

This is unusual in a bedroom so instead of disguising the arch, by using a strong colour it was made into a feature.

How about introducing colour in an unusual way with these fabulous curtain poles, great for a young person's room.

A high ceiling can be painted in a dark colour to create a more intimate space, the end wall of a narrow room painted in a dark colour will give the space more width, whereas light at the furthest visual point draws the eye into the distance. However this can't be achieved if all the walls are the same colour, but when all the walls are dark, it doesn't necessarily mean that the room looks smaller if it is combined with a light coloured flooring and good natural and artificial light.

Intense colour can be used as a focal point as with an accent wall or a back drop to a display of paintings, furniture or a collection of photographs and will draw the attention away from another part of the room that may not be so attractive. Hotels, bars and restaurants cleverly use colour to make the space work for them.

● Colour choices have never been so great as they are today and often that can be quite overwhelming. Modern technology allows us to have almost anything in any colour. However colours do go in and out of fashion just as they do in the clothes industry.

I am sure if I showed you a certain shade of orange and brown in geometric pattern it would remind you of the 1960s or floral pinks and greens on chintz, the 1980s and I am certain we will look back at today's colour choices of neutrals with black accents as the key colour combination of the start of the 21st century. This means if you are choosing colours for a period home then you should research the sort of colours that would have been fashionable then. This is very easy with paint colours for example as many of the paint companies produce a heritage range and even split them into eras such as Regency, Victorian or Georgian. Of course there are certain colours that would not have been available then and if incorporated into a sympathetically restored property may well look out of place. The colours to avoid are white, which has only been available from the 1960s, and any luminous, bright colour that needs petro-chemicals to produce it. Heritage colours tend to be more muted albeit they can still be bold, and the older the property the smaller the range of colours. Stately homes were often decorated in fabulous colours to not only show off their amazing collections of works of art but also to create a mood and character in keeping with the function of that room. If you want to be inspired in how to use colour take advantage of visiting one of our national treasures, a large number of mansions and palaces that reflect an array of historical eras and fashions.

Heritage colours tend to be more muted albeit they can still be bold.

Understanding colour, pattern and fabrics

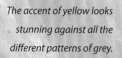

The accent of yellow looks stunning against all the different patterns of grey.

The wide stripped wallpaper here gives this hallway height as well as a distinctive character.

Checks and stripes always work well with plain and other patterned fabrics and furnishings.

Using pattern effectively

Pattern creates variety and interest in almost anything, not just fabrics and wallpaper and we in turn create patterns in the way we display our pictures or arrange our furniture. The pattern maybe small and delicate or loud and extrovert and they all have their place in a well thought out interior design scheme.

- *Pattern should not be thought of in isolation to simply prevent a design scheme looking boring, but as a dynamic addition to your design plans. Don't be drawn to just one pattern as a contrast to everything else being plain, that doesn't create an interesting or exciting room.*

  Pattern is like colour in that the braver you are the more likely you are to combine hugely diverse patterns, but if you are not that way inclined then there are certain patterns that compliment almost any other. That is checks and stripes. They sit very happily against large floral patterns, geometric shapes or picture motifs.

  There is an enormous range of colours and sizes, in fact many fabric manufacturers will often produce co-ordinating checks and stripes to the main fabric. They can also be a great way of pulling together a number of colours that you have used elsewhere.

- *Large patterns are like bold colours, they can dominate a space and bully everything else around it. They can be used as a focal point in a room such as an accent wall, they can be used to alter the proportions of a room or piece of furniture and give that 'wow' factor unique to you.*

  Large patterned wallpaper can also very neatly disguise imperfect walls. However a very large pattern on a very small item can look strange unless the pattern is supposed to be the centrepiece, such as the centre of a cushion.

If your mood board is looking a little bland then it may be lacking some pattern. Pattern on walls and curtains can help change the perspective of a room. Vertical stripes will visually lift a ceiling whilst a horizontal pattern will make the room appear wider.

- *Pattern is a great way of introducing different colours as accents, or continuing the accent colour you have introduced elsewhere. The pattern may not be in the fabric itself but how a variety of finishes have been applied such as a border on a curtain, a trimming on a blind, tassels on a cushion, a grand feather tie back, crystal buttons on a headboard, all can create a subtle but sophisticated look.*

Large patterned wallpaper can also very neatly disguise imperfect walls.

Be careful where you plan to use a pattern.

This beautiful bedroom chair has a subtle pink floral pattern, complemented by the white frame and pink cushion.

Take care not to put too many patterns and finishes together otherwise it might just all look very confusing. Also be careful where you plan to use a pattern, for instance does the wallpaper go round an arch, how will a pattern be affected by a button backed piece of furniture, this is particularly important with any vertical or horizontal patterns. When you are planning curtains or wallpaper be mindful of large pattern repeats which can affect the quantity you will need and hence the costs.

● *Pattern and texture becomes more important where there is a minimal amount of colour to create variety and interest in an interior design scheme. This may be through different types of materials such as leather, silk, velvet, wood, combined in an imaginative way like a patchwork leather rug or a wooden door with metal strips inlaid. Many of the natural materials of course have their own pattern such as a wood grain, or the patina of the leather. Fabrics can have a pattern in the weave such as a damask and velvets can have a cut pattern. Often these types of designs require more planning but the results can be stunning.*

The patterned wallpaper in this neutral colour scheme for a single man creates a fabulous backdrop for plain textured fabrics.

Using fabrics effectively

Whilst your fabric choice should not be the first thing you do in creating your interior design, it is very important in your overall scheme and should be given plenty of thought and consideration.

Fabrics are a great way to look at colour and review how you can combine colours and patterns. In fact, as paint swatches are often too small to really appreciate the full effect of a colour, it is often easier to achieve this with a plain piece of fabric. Fabrics are a great way to explain your ideas to others and for them to share your enthusiasm, see your vision and contribute their own ideas.

There are thousands of fabrics available at a large range of prices. They can be bought from a variety of shops from department stores to specialist fabric shops, as well as from the Internet, exhibitions or design centres. The most important factor with all these is that you do not buy any fabric without seeing it or touching it in the environment for which it is intended. This has already been covered in the mood board section, where the different types of samples available to you can be ordered so that you can see exactly how it will look in your home. Your mood board then allows you to see how it looks with all your other choices. The light and other colours that surround it can seriously affect the look of a fabric, which in the shop may have appeared completely different.

Here are a variety of velvets and texture and pattern can affect the appearance of colour

Laying fabrics together is the only way you can see how well, colour, textures and pattern coordinate.

What is the fabric for?

When you are looking at different fabrics you do need to have some idea of where you are going to use it. To start off with you may just be looking for inspiration, but very quickly you need to be thinking of how and where the fabric is to be used.

Fabrics have many qualities and one of them is their suitability for the role you want them to play. All furnishing fabrics have a series of symbols on their labels that advise you where they can be used in the home. The meaning of each symbol is fairly obvious but if you are not sure then ask for advice.

When you are looking at upholstery fabric the important statistic is its rub count. The higher the number the more durable it will be. For a normal sofa or chair that is used regularly you should look for a minimum rub count of 30,000. This is not so important for an occasional chair or stool where it is more important to look good than have a hard wearing washable cover. There are many natural fabrics, synthetic fabrics and very often a combination of natural and synthetic fabrics to choose from.

Generally synthetic fibres give durability to natural fibres and allows the manufacturers to produce fabrics that can resist stains, be cleaned easier, last longer and often create a variety of colours and textures that can't be achieved with natural fibres alone.

Consider carefully where the fabric is to be used and how the environment might affect it. Sunlight will eventually fade all fabrics but silk will fade quicker and can rot in the sun. Silk is a beautiful fabric, it is opulent, it reflects light and comes in a large range of colours and finishes, so if you want to use it as a window dressing, take advice from your curtain maker. A light coloured fabric, which is going to be constantly touched or brushes the floor will probably look grubby quicker than a dark patterned fabric and therefore limit its useful life. This doesn't mean you shouldn't use it, it only means that you should make an informed choice.

This is a simple colour scheme that shows off the patterned fabric and wallpaper beautifully.

Interior Design Secrets . . . .

The quantity and impact of your fabric

The impact of a fabric differs considerably depending on how much of it is to be used. If you have chosen a vibrant strong colour as your accent colour against a neutral background then it is important to know how you plan to introduce it. You may choose to use the brightly coloured fabric for your cushions, lampshades or table runner only, in which case you may only need a small amount to give the "wow" factor. (Of course your accent colour doesn't have to be a fabric it might be a paint effect, a carpet or rug or even a colour in your paintings.)

However, the fabric you are considering may be a significant part of your overall design. You may have a room with many windows and therefore the curtain material is very important to the overall look. You may have decided to line the walls with fabric; tent a ceiling or maybe the upholstered furniture is to be the focal point of the room. In this case your fabric will be very dominant and it has a huge impact on your choice of the design, colour and texture of the material in terms of the size of your room and what else is in it.

When you are compiling your mood board it is recommended that the quantity of fabric displayed on it should be represented in the ratios in which you intend to use them. If there is an expensive fabric that you would love to use but is out of your budget for you to be able to use in large quantities, then why not use it as an impact fabric? You could just cover one chair in it, use it on some decorative pillowcases or if it is really stunning, maybe frame it as a picture. Don't dismiss it because you are not able to use it for your curtains.

This gorgeous cushion and crystal button steals the show when set against the background of a red chair

The vibrant red velvet of this chair picks up the red highlights in the picture above.

Bringing variety into your choice

A variety of fabrics makes a scheme a lot more interesting and are often used to achieve that "wow" factor. If you are choosing fabrics that are fairly neutral in colour then variety can be introduced through texture and pattern, again by putting them together on your mood board you will be able to judge if your selection creates the spark you are looking for. In my experience most people are fearful of colour and pattern and end up playing it safe. By putting together a mood board you are able to experiment with some unusual combinations before having to commit to any significant expenditure. It is all about having fun, and if you have had fun pulling your design together then others will have fun looking at it.

Getting help in the shop

It is very easy to feel intimidated in a fabric shop when someone asks you what you are looking for if you haven't got a clue. However a sales assistant can be very helpful if you are able to clearly give her your ideas based on your mood board. She may well be able to suggest fabrics that you wouldn't have ordinarily considered, she will certainly be able to point you in the right direction as many of the fabric shops have more fabric choices than you would ever have time or energy to properly consider.

This mood board is for a traditional dining room and contains ideas as well as fabric swatches for the style and colour theme in the room.

Being budget conscious

Fabric is only one element of your cost so please remember that unless you are able to make or upholster all your furnishings then a significant cost will be the labour.

There are many ways in which to control your fabric budget and you will find whoever makes your soft furnishings for you can give you advice on all your options and their respective costs. Remember that a large pattern repeat will increase the quantity of fabric needed to make anything whether it is curtains, upholstery or simply a bed cover and this affects the price. If you discover that there is a lot of wastage when your soft furnishings are being made then think about how you can use what is left over, maybe for cushions for example. Inexpensive fabrics can be decorated with braids, beads or fringes to produce something that looks much more expensive. For example plain curtain fabrics can have a contrast border, different curtain headings use different quantities of fabric or you could have a blind with dress curtains to create a beautiful look that limits the amount of fabric required. It has already been mentioned that impact fabrics can completely change a design. A bedroom can be transformed by adding a pair of stunning cushions and a bed throw to plain bed linen. A kitchen can be given interest with an exciting roman blind, or a plain threepiece suite lifted by some exotic cushions.

It is not always what you choose but how you choose to use it. Sometimes a limited budget encourages you to be more imaginative. In my experience it is better to have beautifully made soft furnishings from less expensive fabric than prioritising the fabric and compromising on the quality of workmanship. Certainly the difference between handmade curtains and those you can buy in a shop is immeasurable.

This blind only required one width of fabric as the contrast border widened the blind to match the required measurements.

'The wallpaper in this room tied all the colours together and the pattern created interest and a focal point.

Understanding colour, pattern and fabrics

*This group of different patterned
fabrics work well together as they all
use the same colour palette.*

Using heritage style fabrics

Different styles have different patterns and proportions; which is why you need to ensure you understand exactly the overall style that meets your personality and tastes and that of the property. A classic French style has dainty, ornate furniture with bow legs and delicate decoration with soft muted colours and pretty patterns. A country house style is chunky and heavy with earthy colours and traditional patterns such as checks. A minimalist style will be understated, plain, often without pattern and use very modern materials such as plastics.

If you have a period property and you are wanting to be sympathetic to its heritage, then different periods also have their own respective shapes and sizes, a 1930s house will be very angular with Art Deco influences, whilst an Arts and Crafts home will have organic and fluid shapes. So whilst you are considering the proportions of everything in your home they need to be seen within the context of your overall style. Even if you are going for an eclectic look the respective proportions and scale are just as important. Remember that an eclectic look is not just one piece of furniture that doesn't match, that will just look like a mistake, an eclectic look needs to be planned so that whilst there will be plenty of variety there is still harmony.

Modern fabrics, paints and wallpapers are nowadays readily available to all of us. The range of colours especially, has only been a recent development with the use of industrial chemicals and processes.

Historically, colours would have been muted as only natural dyes were available for natural fabrics, wool for the common man and silk and velvets for the gentry. When cotton mills became commonplace during the industrial revolution they started to give greater versatility to the fabric industry with cheaper materials, which were easier to dye and sew. Then finally with the development of the petro-chemical industry and the invention of nylon (invented in New York and London, hence it's name) and more recently polyester, the fabric sector was transformed.

Historically any patterns on the fabric were either woven in or embroidered decoration, with mainly floral patterns, which would have been expensive and only accessible to the wealthy few. Now with the ability to print and dye anything on any fabric including synthetic material gives us the most amazing choice.

Many of the fabric houses own original prints and patterns and they are regularly re-launched, sometimes using new colours or with larger or smaller patterns. Sanderson now owns all the William Morris designs for instance, and they have a separate William Morris collection. Morris as an artist and designer was a leading light in the Arts and Crafts movement at the beginning of the twentieth century. Although these fabrics are from a different time period they can still look fabulous in a modern home. It all depends where it is used and how it is combined with other fabrics. There are other fabric companies that have similar collections using historical archives and depending on the fashion trends will re-issue them fairly regularly.

This modern heraldic fabric was chosen for a study in a seventeenth century country house for its masculine sense and heritage look.

At the moment there is a great 1950's retro revival, which can be clearly seen in the latest fabric launches. If you are looking for a period look and you are not sure where to start then take a look at some of our historical homes. You will notice that it is not just the fabric itself that is important but also how it has been dressed. You will probably find large quantities of fabric with bullion fringes or other decoration to give a rich, opulent feel that would have impressed any guests. Whilst you may not wish to have swags and tails adorning your windows, you can still develop a similar look and feel, if that is the character you are wishing to create, through the richness and colour of the fabric chosen.

Sometimes, as I have mentioned previously, we have too great a choice. It would be very difficult today not to find a fabric that is beautiful, suitable and at the appropriate price. Fabrics that are still embellished in some way with embroidery, beading and ribbons will still be more expensive than the plain fabrics or printed ones reflecting the amount of work that has gone into making them.

This brings us back to the beginning of the book where we talked about giving your home a character this also applies in a period property. An elegant, smart or quirky style can be incorporated into an historical setting. Don't be completely limited by the colours and patterns of a particular era, but it can be a great place to start for inspiration, especially if you are struggling with ideas for colours and patterns.

This red silk curtain has been given a regal makeover with the choice of trimmings and tie back.

Interior Design Secrets . . . .

HOT TIPS

It is important not to be fearful of colour but embrace what it can do for your Interior Design scheme. It can create ambience, a focal point, visual space and be a backdrop to your beautiful objects.

If you are unsure of how to combine colour then the rules of the colour wheel can be a good place to start.

If bold colours scare you then introduce them as accents to provide depth and interest to your scheme.

Pattern is as important as colour in the way you introduce it to your design. All patterns look great alongside stripes and checks, so don't restrict yourself to one pattern style.

A pattern can be natural, as with the grain in wood or created by adding a finish to something, such as a border to a blind. There is pattern in the way something is arranged or organised, for instance, furniture layout, laying of tiles or display of pictures.

There aren't many rooms where we don't use fabric and the choices are enormous. Choose your fabric carefully, not just for its colour and design, but also for its price and suitability. Always collect a sample for your mood board.

Colours, patterns, types and style of fabrics have changed greatly over time with fashion and technology. If you are re-furbishing a period property then many fabric and paint manufacturers have heritage ranges that can steer you in the right direction.

Strong colours used subtlely can create a powerful impact in a room.

6

Understanding the impact of light and lighting

Quite often the difference between a professional interior design scheme and one created by the average home owner is the emphasis put on the importance of lighting. A well thought out lighting plan can be one of the most effective ways of bringing out the best in a room. It can highlight precious ornaments, disguise irregularities, create a warm intimate atmosphere or a positive vibrant ambience. All this can be achieved in one room.

The style of house can make a great deal of difference in the amount of light available in an interior. City flats may enjoy little naturally available light and be overlooked on all sides and a country cottage with low ceilings and tiny windows can seem dark and gloomy even on a sunny day, whereas a living room with a patio or conservatory is exposed to the continuing changes in light and the lighting scheme needs to accommodate this.

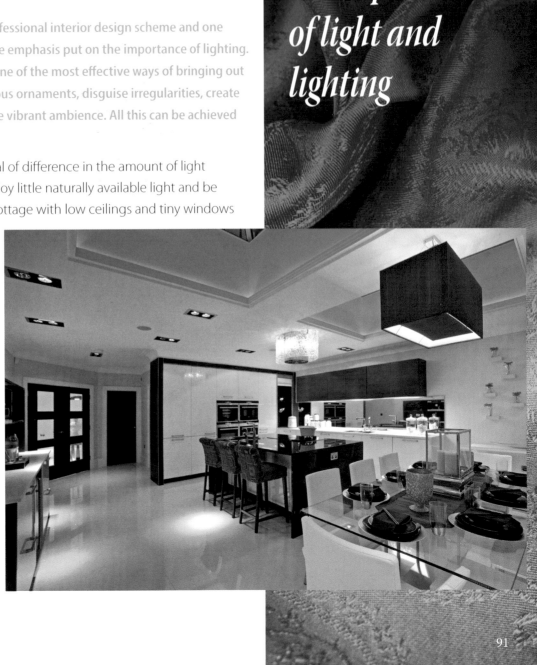

There is evidence to suggest that the quality of light has a direct impact on our levels of concentration and comfort too so that different spaces require different lighting solutions. The most practical way of achieving this is to have good, general background lighting supplemented by lighting directed at particular parts of a room, which can be brought into use as and when necessary.

Bedside lamps are practical so why not make them stylish too.

Task lighting is easy to understand and very important in certain rooms.

The five different categories of lighting

Lighting can be simply separated into five categories

1 **Background lighting:** this is the minimum type of lighting required, which enables you to see your surroundings and gives a general light that creates an ambience. Until very recently, for many this was the only lighting option available with one central pendant light in a room.

2 **Task lighting:** this is easy to understand and very important in certain rooms. This is a directional light over a surface where you will perform a task, it may be a work surface in a kitchen, a desk in a studio, or a reading chair in a library. This lighting should not produce glare, or cast shadows as this will cause eye strain, and the type of task will dictate the amount of light needed. The recent development in LED downlighters has made it a lot easier to achieve a small directional pool of light from almost anywhere onto almost any surface.

3 **Decorative lighting:** this defines lighting that is beautiful to look at as well as lighting that accents something fabulous that you want to highlight. In this category it would include chandeliers, gorgeous lamps, sculptural wall lights and any light that commands your attention and may even be a focal point in a room. Then there are small spots of light that draw your attention to a fantastic design such as beautiful curtains, an inherited painting, a display of treasured items or just anything that you love. The light may come from below, to the side or above, it is only limited by your imagination and budget.

4 **Safety lighting:** this is very important especially on stairs and in entrances, however it does not have to be boring. Well-placed lighting can emphasise a pleasing staircase, or an interesting archway and at the same time increase the feeling of space. In this category it is essential to have the light switches in the correct position for entering and exiting these important connecting spaces and it will often mean two-way switches are needed. Also remember water and electricity don't mix, so in wet areas there are strict rules in the positioning of all electrical points.

5 **Mood lighting:** this enables you to change the mood of the room simply through altering the light. This is particularly useful in rooms that perform more than one function, such as a kitchen/diner or in a room where you may entertain, relax and work. This can be achieved by layering light, so that different combinations can be used for different occasions and the use of dimmers can alter the subtlety and intensity of the light, for example you would not want to have a candlelit dinner under a strip light.

Style of lighting

How do you decide which style of lighting to choose? We have already looked at the different categories of lighting, (background, task, decorative, safety and mood) but certain styles of lighting can perform more than one function, for example a lamp can be both decorative, task and contribute to the background lighting.

After deciding how you are going to use the room and therefore where you need the light, then the next important factor is the size of the room. If the room is small with low ceilings, then decorative pendant lighting won't be practical and there may not be enough room for lamps that need to be placed on furniture. However

Mood lighting enables you to change the mood of the room simply through altering the light.

downlighters that take up no space within the room and would work beautifully, wall lights and a floor lamp can allow you to layer your lighting (see the Layering light section later in this chapter) as well as creating variety and interest in your design scheme.

Conversely if you have a large entrance and hallway, you may want to make a grand statement with a fabulous pendant light, modern or traditional, that may be the focal point in that space, but may not give enough light for safety reasons on the stairs. LED lighting allows you to be far more imaginative than just supplementing with downlighters. You can light the steps or have small lights in or above the skirting board lighting each step or every other step, or even light the underneath of the stair bannister to wash the stairs in light. You can have wall washer lights, these are wall lights that wash the wall with light, up, down or in both directions and they create a combination of light and shade on the wall. You may have pictures or paintings on the wall and picture lights can not only light up the art work but also contribute to the overall lighting mood of the room.

ABOVE:

This neat wall light with a directional arm looks great and saves space.

LEFT:

This modern take on a chandelier looks great in a dining room with a low ceiling.

Interior Design Secrets . . . .

If you have a dining room where you would like to have a large central light but the room isn't big enough to take one, consider having three smaller pendant lights in a row, this works particularly well in a kitchen diner, where you want to light the kitchen table independently. You could also have a group of pendant lights that hang at different lengths and are of varying sizes above a kitchen island to create a fascinating focal point. As with other grouped objects, they look best if they have something in common such as shape or colour, and be careful not to overdo it.

If there is very limited space either side of the bed for bedside lamps, there are wall lights on arms or with a separate spot, or even more exciting have a pendant light either side of the headboard hanging over the bedside table with a mirror on the wall behind them to give an exciting solution to a practical problem.

Lighting within furniture is nothing new, but lit floors are. They have been used in the commercial world for quite a while but have generally only been used in very modern industrial style domestic designs. There is no reason why you shouldn't consider it for a bathroom, hallway, especially if it connects unusual spaces or even a dining room. It would be a brave choice, however it would certainly give you that unique 'wow' factor. Hotels and restaurants are great places for sources of inspiration in how to light a room, look at the mood that they have created, intimate, lively, calm and then see how they have achieved it for a particular style: modern, historical or ethnic. The lighting will be both discreet and decorative and often layered in imaginative ways.

LED lamps allows for greater flexibility in where lights can be positioned.

Layering light

The right lighting can change a mood in a room, can allow a room to be used for different purposes and can change the focal point.

Having different layers of lighting essentially means being able to operate different lights independently, for example wall lights and ceiling lights would have separate switches so that they can either be used together or separately and if the switches are dimmable then the flexibility in changing the quality of the light improves greatly. The right lighting can change a mood in a room, can allow a room to be used for different purposes and can change the focal point. This flexibility, as our chosen way of living is moving towards open plan, is a great way of defining areas too. The other advantage of layering light is that when you are choosing a style of light you don't have to make so many compromises in order for your chosen style of light to perform several functions. So the beautiful lamps, or sculptural wall lights that you have fallen in love with can be supplemented with downlighters or pendant lights or the extravagant chandelier can be added to by spots or some well chosen floor lamps.

When designing a lighting plan, layering the various types of light mentioned above is the key. It is important to plan your lighting and don't automatically accept what is already there.

The size and quantity of lighting needs to be in proportion to the room and the furniture within it. Too much light will be overbearing and not enough will make the room feel gloomy and depressing. Your lighting plan needs to be unique to each room but you may well have a common theme or style that continues throughout your home. This will often depend on the style of the property and of course your taste. If it is an older property and especially if it is listed you may well have physical stylistic limitations that should be discussed with a qualified electrician and may need to be approved by English Heritage.

Light, lighting and colour

Natural light is constantly changing according to whether it is sunny or dull, and it varies in intensity throughout the day and with the seasons. It's also worth noting that the quality of light in different parts of the world will have a bearing on your choice of design scheme, especially the colours, so that certain colours look fabulous in strong sunlight but can look jaded or garish in our Northern European light. The effect of light on colour is called metamerism, which is when two items look the same under one light source such as daylight, but change dramatically when viewed under a different light source such as incandescent lighting

Lighting by Porta Romana.

When light strikes an object, certain waves of light are absorbed by the object. The other waves are reflected back to us. These light waves, which are reflected back, determine what colour we perceive the object to be. In a dark room, we do not see colours, but as the light increases, the same object will appear to be in different colours under different degrees of light.

The direction in which the room is facing is another factor, whether the room is facing, north, south, east or west makes a great deal of difference in the quality of the light at different times of the day. For example a bedroom that faces east and receives strong sunlight in the early morning will look very different when seen late at night in artificial light and a west facing room that has a warm glow in the evening can look dull in the mornings. As a general rule a northern light adds blue to a colour, east adds green, south adds yellow-white and washes out colour, while west adds orange. Therefore an orange colour scheme in a west facing room in the afternoon light may be a bit too overpowering for example.

We know that lighting affects colour, so it is very important that any colours you are considering are viewed in the room for which they are intended, in natural and

Northern light adds blue to a colour, east adds green, south adds yellow-white, while west adds orange.

A combination of downlighters and lamps creates pools of light to highlight different features.

The smoother the surface of an object, the more it will reflect light and the more intense the colour will appear.

artificial light. Once you have a good idea of the colours you wish to use, the fabric, wallpaper and paint colours need to be put in position in the room and lived with for a few days. They should be distributed throughout the room where the light differs, for example if you are painting a room, paint a sample patch by the window and in the corner furthest away from natural light and somewhere in between so that you can see how they look in day and electric light. Make sure that the patch is big enough to create the best effect, I would suggest at least a square metre and apply at least two coats to see the true colour. Of course this isn't possible if the room is yet to be built but you can probably simulate the same effect elsewhere. You can always create large painted boards that be transported and reviewed where possible. In general the different times of the day have the following effect on colour:

- *Morning light – cool daylight absorbs the coolness and shifts colour towards warmer pigments,*
- *Strong daylight – very bright direct sunlight washes out colour and lightens and whitens it,*
- *Faded daylight – mixed light cancels both warm and cool tones making a colour duller and neutral,*
- *Artificial light – warm light absorbs warming pigments moving the colour to a cooler effect.*

As well as the direction of the room another consideration is what part of the day is the room generally used? Is it a dining room usually used in the evening and will generally be lit by artificial light or is it a playroom or study, normally used during the day and the quality of natural light is important. This is another benefit in creating a mood board so that all your chosen colours can be seen in the light of your home at the particular time of day that the room will be used. So for example, if you have chosen rich deep colours for a dining room, you need to make sure they look their best in the evening with your chosen artificial lighting, as opposed to the way they looked in the showroom. You will be surprised how different a colour can look in artificial light and away from bright shop spotlights.

The smoother the surface of an object, the more it will reflect light and the more intense the colour will appear. The more irregular the surface, the less it will reflect light and the lesser the intensity of the colour. A textured fabric will look slightly less intense than a silky fabric of the same colour against the same background. So the effect of not just the light but also the material will have an impact on the colour seen.

There are so many factors that influence the final appearance of the colour that you can't always count on the colour rules to guide you. Sometimes you must rely on your trained eye to tell you whether a particular colour scheme works in a particular situation.

Light and space

Use of light can either attract the eye towards desirable features, or distract it from less desirable aspects, and a well lit point in a room dictates where the eye is drawn. Often in hotels at the end of a corridor there will be a painting with a bright picture light that distracts you from thinking about the length of the corridor and creates interest in what is happening at the end. You could create the same effect with a brightly lit picture at the end of a narrow hallway that lacks natural light or a large mirror with light bouncing of it. You may have downlighters angled on fabulous curtains, a fireplace or a piece of artwork, that detracts from ugly doors or unusual dimensions. It is just a matter of guiding the eye to where you want it to go. Think of a spotlight on a stage, this is creating the same effect.

Downlighters angled on fabulous curtains, a fireplace or a piece of artwork, that detracts from ugly doors or unusual dimensions.

Mirrors are a great way of increasing the light in any room and look elegant too.

The light may be a focal point of the room as for example a large chandelier or a pair of beautiful table lamps. However in small spaces or low ceilings creating good light can be a problem. Wall lights can be a good alternative, although if this is the only light source it does mean all the light will be pooled around the edge of a room. However these can work very well with some downlighters discretely placed. Downlighters are lights that aren't there to be looked at but they are used to create pools of light in the right places.

Reflective materials can also add light and space. A mirror is an obvious way in which to bring in more light and give the impression of more space but this effect can be created with other shiny surfaces. Besides mirrored furniture, which is very popular, there are also reflective wallpapers, glossy furniture, glass and plastic furniture that not only reflect light but can visually look smaller. A glass dining room table, although a large piece of furniture, takes up little visual space as you can see through it. Bathroom and kitchen cupboards that are suspended above the floor also take up less visual space as you can see the floor continue underneath, this is very effective in small rooms.

ABOVE: *Bathroom by Versace.*

LEFT:

This cloakroom has no natural light so all the reflective surfaces help amplify the central pendant light.

A light colour will never come to life in a dark room.

What do you do with a small space with very poor light or even no natural light. Well it is the opposite to what you would expect, a light colour will never come to life in a dark room, but a rich, deep colour can make a dim sombre space feel warm and luminous even though it receives no natural light.

Understanding the impact of light and lighting

Lit mirrors in a bathroom are a great way of introducing task lighting into a bathroom.

Plan your lighting

Any major changes to your current lighting arrangements will almost certainly mean some channelling walls or cutting and repairing holes in the ceiling. If this is part of a major refurbishment, then make sure you discuss it with your builder upfront as any later changes will be costly. If this is part of a redecorating project then it should be one of the first changes to be made and a qualified electrician will be able to give you guidelines on the amount of artificial light a room will need, you will then have to decide how to distribute this among the various light sources. This just further re-enforces the importance of planning, with a clear idea of who and how the space is going to be used you can plan your lighting requirements accordingly.

Lighting technology

Dimmer switches work by cutting the voltage passing through a light bulb, this will not only cut down on the amount of electricity used, but also prolong the life of the bulb. Dimmers change the colour of light and emphasise the golden-red end of the colour spectrum, and therefore atmospheric room settings can be created by just using careful adjustments of the dimmer switch. The switches are easy to install and it is possible to wire them to all kinds of fittings, from floor and table lights to ceiling and wall lights. Task lights that have a dimmer switch can contribute to the mood and ambience lighting as well.

Long lasting light bulbs are replacing the traditional ones to reduce the carbon footprint of our homes. These lights can often give a completely different light quality from previously, so research carefully the quantity, quality and colour of the light before purchasing a light bulb, you may find that you will need to supplement your lighting. Buy one and try it out. There are websites that have reviewed all the different options, **goodhousekeeping.com** has a good summary both pictorially and with statistics comparing the various light bulbs on offer.

LED lights are replacing halogen lights most commonly used in downlighters. Although the bulbs are three to four times more expensive, some have an average lifetime of 50,000 hours. Which means that if a light bulb was left on for 24 hours, 7 days a week it would last for over 6 years. Their low voltage means that they don't heat up like halogen bulbs and with the associated reduced fire risk, they can be installed in areas previously not possible. This can be very useful in older properties where clear space in ceilings and floors have hitherto been too small and accommodating modern lighting discreetly has been a challenge.

Light fittings

There are large ranges of light fittings available. There are some that replicate the look and feel of candlelight with a rustic feel whilst others that have been designed in a classical theme in style, colour and presentation and then there are modern sleek interpretations of a traditional look as well as the very modern funky styles. Light fittings, like anything else, can be made bespoke to incorporate a design relevant to your property. A light fitting can be a work of art and may be at the centre of your design scheme.

A light fitting can be a work of art and may be at the centre of your design scheme.

Lighting by Serip.

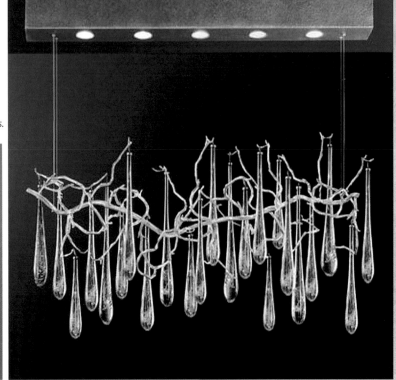

Examples of contrasting lighting styles.

Understanding the impact of light & lighting
HOT TIPS

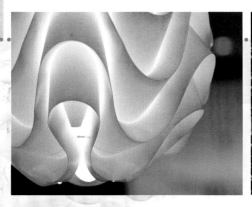

Lighting plans are essential for the overall success of your interior design scheme. Professional interior designers have this high on their design list requirements.

Lighting basically comes in five different types: background, task, decorative, safety and mood. To create flexibility with your lighting, the trick is to layer these various types.

There are a great many styles of lighting available that can be modern, colourful, heritage, made from different materials and of varying sizes, which can be combined and layered with stunning effects.

Light affects colour whether it is natural or artificial so it is very important that you see your chosen paint and fabrics in the light of the room for which it is intended.

Lighting has gone through great changes lately, especially in the area of saving energy but the effect can be different from what you are used to so try out various options.

7

Understanding design principles

When you know the basic interior design principles you can transform any space to look fabulous. You know what it feels like when you walk into a well-designed room. You can sense how everything feels cohesive and well put together. It just feels right. You can achieve that effect in your own home with a little knowledge of basic design principles. Pair that knowledge with practice and experimentation and you are on your way to creating a beautiful home.

There are many design principles that interior designers use when designing a home, and in this chapter we are going to look at the following important ones:

- Scale
- Proportion
- Balance
- Focal Point
- Rhythm
- Harmony

The first three are important when it comes to the layout of a room and its furniture: scale, proportion and balance. These terms are used interchangeably in the design world and they can be confused, but in fact they are quite different.

Architectural spaces that are intended to impress us are usually scaled to a size that would dwarf the human viewer.

Scale

In simple terms scale refers to the overall size of an object in relation to what we might consider "the norm". For example the scale of a sofa is either small or large when compared to our idea of a "standard sized sofa".

If you walked into a friend's small apartment and they had one of those overstuffed, lounging sectional sofas, you would be right in thinking that the sofa was too large for the space, in other words out of scale. The same could apply to a large king-sized bed that fills a tiny bedroom or perhaps a massive flat screen television that overshadows the fireplace mantle next to it, or even a lampshade that is far too big for its base.

Scale is often determined by the size of the room. A large-scale room will require large-scale furniture. Whatever style you choose the pieces of furniture need to be an appropriate scale for the setting. For instance if you have high ceilings, large windows and doors, then choose a large sofa, a bed with a large headboard or a big roll top bath to stop these pieces looking lost within the space. Likewise if you have low ceilings with beams, you may want to choose a low backed sofa, a low hall console table, or a simply designed chair in the corner of the room.

Architectural spaces that are intended to impress us are usually scaled to a size that would dwarf the human viewer. Public spaces, such as churches or government buildings, corporate spaces and museums are often very large in scale relative to other buildings. These structures impress us with their grandeur and size, creating a sense of power and invincibility. In contrast, the much smaller scale of a house makes it appear friendlier, more comfortable and less intimidating.

So where do you start? The obvious starting point is with the size of the room, the height of the ceilings, the size of the windows and any other architectural feature such as doors, fireplaces, covings and skirting boards. Is the scale appropriate for the size of the room? It can be difficult to change the size of windows and doors in particular, but the way they are decorated and dressed can change the appearance of their size. For instance, the size of the door handle, any beading or the architrave around the door can change its appearance, or using full length curtains with a pelmet can make a window seem bigger. Changing the depth of coving and skirting boards can change the apparent height of a ceiling as can the colour that they are painted. If they are the same colour or very similar to that of the walls they will form a visual part of the wall and can help lift a low ceiling. Conversely, using a contrasting colour can make a ceiling feel lower. When you are visiting places like bars, restaurants, museums or hotels, see if you can see how they have tricked the eye into thinking the size of space is different from what it is in reality and think about how you can do the same in your home.

The style of furniture will often affect its scale. The materials used and the colour can influence its visual size so that for example a mirrored or glass piece of furniture will look smaller than something made of dark wood. Glass tables, which are currently very popular for that very reason, allow you to have a relatively large piece of furniture without it appearing to dominate the space.

This lamp is out of scale with the rest of the furniture which is why it doesn't look right.

Whilst this a beautiful hallway the proportions of the mirror aren't in keeping with the proportions of the room so that it looks too small for the wall space.

Proportion is important because it creates a little spot of harmony,

Proportion

Proportion refers to the relative size and scale of the various elements. It explains the relationship of the size of all the objects as well as between one part of an object and another, in the room. A good example is the way furniture is designed. If the legs of a table aren't in correct proportion to the top, the table could just look silly. Or if the arms of the sofa are over or undersized, the sofa is uncomfortable and unattractive.

Proportion is important because each time it is used correctly, it creates a little spot of harmony, if not it looks and feels wrong. This doesn't just apply to pieces of furniture, but also to patterns, colours and lighting.

Once you understand the proportions of the room then you need to look at the proportions of the articles in the room. Obviously this in part will be dictated by how you use the space. If it is a bedroom you may have to accommodate a double bed, if it is a lounge then you may need to be able to seat five people at one time. All of this will influence the choice of furniture.

Items such as lamps, pictures and occasional furniture need to be in proportion with the major items in the room. If you are planning to have a side table either

Interior Design Secrets . . . .

side of a large sofa with a lamp on each table, then the lamps also need to be large with impressive shades to complement and not be dominated by the sofa. This also applies to pictures, although you can group pictures together closely to give the same effect as one large picture. The architects of our grand stately homes understood clearly the principles of scale and proportion and everything was made or designed for a particular space within the room.

Some proportional relationships are more pleasing than others. The ancient Greeks came up with the Golden Rectangle or Mean, which sought to reduce all proportion to a simple formula: the ratio of the smaller section to the larger section should be the same as that of the larger section to the whole. This they calculated to be 2:3 ratio which is present in nature, and artists and architects have used it as well. The 2:3 ratio translates to 4 x 6, 8 x 12, 16 x 24 etc. You will probably recognize those dimensions as common in picture frames, rug sizes, table sizes etc. While the calculation may seem complicated your eye will determine whether something is in proportion or not as it will feel uncomfortable and unattractive, even if you can't quite put your finger on why. According to the Greeks, a square is the least pleasing proportion, which is why you very rarely see a square room.

'Less is more', is a phrase used very often, but what does it actually mean and how does that apply to an interior design scheme? Many people are afraid of buying accessories that are too big, so they take a conservative view, buy something smaller and then when they have it in the home, they feel there is something missing. So to fill in the space they buy other things.

The 'less is more' principle is explained by buying only one item that is big enough to occupy and own the space, rather than buying many items. This can apply to a mirror or a painting on a wall, a rug on a floor, pillows on a bed or something as simple as a door-knocker on a front door. It is very fashionable to have things oversized rather than too small and fewer of them. If you are uncomfortable or unsure about the impact a large item will have in a room, then cut out a template in newspaper and put it where your item will be placed to get a feel of how it will look with regard to size. It is better to invest in one large item rather than many small ones as not only can it be less expensive, but it will also have a greater impact. It will also steer you away from cluttering up a room.

According to the Greeks, a square is the least pleasing proportion, which is why you very rarely see a square room.

Chippenham, Langley Burrell.

The organisation of your furniture and accessories can change the harmony and balance in a room.

Balance

How do they make the rooms in the magazines look so good? The answer to this lies in not only about the individual pieces that have been chosen but also how they have been arranged. The organisation of your furniture and accessories can change the harmony and balance in a room. You would never consider putting all your furniture at one end of the room, that would be an impractical use of the space, but by creating a furniture plan you will ensure that not only will your room be in balance, but you will also buy the right sized furniture.

In design, balance creates a feeling of equilibrium. It is about equalising or approximating the visual weight of objects. Interior spaces contain various elements, each with its own visual weight determined by shape, colour, size and texture. Certain characteristics enhance or increase the visual weight of an object and attract attention to it:

- Irregular or contrasting shapes
- Bright colours
- Contrasting textures
- Large dimensions and unusual proportions
- Elaborate details

If you want to design a successful interior, you need to balance all the different elements contained in it. Balance is a design principle that deals with equilibrium, so to achieve balance you need to equally distribute visual weight in the space. Since interiors are three dimensional, you should think of visual balance in three dimensions.

There are three kinds of balance:

- Symmetrical
- Asymmetrical
- Radial

Interior Design Secrets . . . .

Symmetrical balance

You obtain symmetrical balance when you arrange identical elements in the same position on either side of an imaginary axis, in other words, you divide the space in two, and arrange objects in the same way on each side, so that they are a mirror image of each other.

This is very easy to achieve and understand, symmetrical balance conveys a feeling of calm, security, formality and stability and it is a simple yet powerful way to achieve visual order. However symmetry extended to the whole interior is too much, and can give it a conventional and boring look. You are better off creating local symmetrical groupings within the room, this way, you simplify and organise the composition without making it look too formal.

You will nearly always see a display of objects, in adverts and magazines, arranged symmetrically. There will be a chair either side of the window with a vase of flowers on top of an occasional table between the chairs. There will be a chest of drawers with a picture placed centrally above it with a pair of candlesticks either side or two matching sofas either side of a fireplace with a coffee table in the middle.

Symmetrical balance conveys a feeling of calm, security, formality and stability.

India Jane.

We love symmetry; it creates an order and balance that is pleasing to the eye. Apparently the most beautiful faces are perfectly symmetrical, our bodies are symmetrical, nature is symmetrical, animals, flowers, trees; they all have symmetry. In symmetry there is balance; which gives order to a room and that in turn gives a sense of calm and space. If that is really important to you in your interior design scheme then carefully plan how you will create symmetry.

In order to create real symmetry then everything needs to be arranged in odd numbers, that is one item in the centre with an even number of items either side. That is why a mirror with two lamps either side is a common display, two chairs either side of a side table, candle sticks either side of a painting above the mantel piece all create a classically interesting arrangement. Arranging and displaying items in threes is a magical formula in interior design. You can create a triangle where either the item in the middle is higher than that either side of it or the reverse, where the item in the middle is smaller and create an inverted triangle. Triangles have been important symbols throughout history so it is not surprising that they work well within our homes.

If you look at stately homes, symmetry was paramount in everything in the building. The architectural design would have followed a mathematical formula to ensure, the grounds, the building and its rooms conformed to a regular pattern. This can more easily be seen in their display of paintings. The architect would have planned exactly how many paintings were to be hung, their relative sizes with the largest one being above the fireplace; which of course was in the centre of the wall. The paintings would then have been commissioned to fit exactly its allotted space. Even the furniture would have been designed and arranged for that particular room giving it perfect symmetry and balance. The façades of these homes were always designed to be symmetrical so that they were impressive and beautiful. In the Royal Crescent in Bath, one of the most magnificent streets in England, it is only the front of the buildings that are perfectly symmetrical. Behind the façade you purchased your piece of land and you were allowed to build whatever you could afford, so the rear of this street is anything but symmetrical. However the town planners of the day wanted the appearance of symmetry and order in their city.

> *In symmetry there is balance; which gives order to a room and that in turn gives a sense of calm and space.*

Interior Design Secrets . . . .

The arrangement of the pictures creates balance with the mirror and window to create an interesting arrangement in a bathroom.

Asymmetrical balance

Symmetry is easy to create if the room allows it but what do you do if the architectural features of the room aren't balanced? The fireplace may not be in the centre of the wall or the doors and windows are not exactly where you would have wanted them to be if you were planning the room from scratch. This is particularly common in homes that have been extended where walls have been removed and the function of the room has changed.

However there are visual tricks you can play to create visual balance. For example an off-centre window can be counter balanced with a large mirror, a door in the corner can be balanced with a picture above a side table, an off-centre fireplace can be centralised with a chair to one side to even up the space, a rug can be placed in such a way to move the visual centre of a room and the use of fabrics can even up different sized windows.

There are visual tricks you can play to create visual balance.

Understanding design principles

If you want to achieve asymmetrical balance, you need to take into account the visual weight of each element.

This is called asymmetrical balance, which brings into equilibrium elements that have the same visual weight, but are different in shape, size or colour and texture, they are equivalent but not identical. If you want to achieve asymmetrical balance, you need to take into account the visual weight of each element and use the principle of leverage in their arrangement. To do this, you counterbalance elements that have a great visual weight and attract attention, like bright colours, dark shapes, heavy texture and unusual shapes with visually lighter elements that either are larger in size or grouped together.

Pictures and mirrors in particular are an easy way to create balance. Asymmetrical balance can be achieved for example by using a pair of pictures, one above another to balance a door the other side of a fireplace, a mirror can help balance an off-centre window, in fact using asymmetry in the way you place objects is a great way to disguise quirky architectural features that you have inherited. Likewise, objects don't have to be identical, you can have two lamps that aren't exactly the same shape but they are nearly the same size, two chairs covered in different patterned fabrics that are the same colour, a candlestick balanced by a sculpture on top of a fireplace that is roughly the same size. Indeed by items not being exactly the same you can create interest whilst still maintaining an orderly balance and adding your personal flair. If you are having trouble creating that balanced, harmonious look then consider how you can re-arrange your items that gives as much balance as your room will allow. If you have pairs of objects scattered around the house, now may be a time to re-unite them. Lighting can also help by giving emphasis to a part of the room that may be naturally dark, or by giving light either side of a focal point in the room, such as lamps on top of bedside cabinets either side of the bed.

Another way to display something asymmetrically is with one item. This could be a large sculpture on one side of the mantelpiece above a fireplace. It could be a large lamp in the corner curving over a sofa or a grandfather clock at one end of the hallway. Displaying a single item asymmetrically can be a style statement, creating a 'wow' factor with its simplicity and drama. It must be deliberate and not look as if something is missing and can be a great way to create an unusual focal point, especially if it is large and unique.

Although more difficult to achieve, asymmetrical balance is dynamic, informal and visually active, it can express movement, change and spontaneity, and is certainly more interesting than symmetrical balance when it is done well.

Radial Balance

In radial balance, you arrange elements around a centre point. The elements can face inwards towards the centre, or outwards from the centre. An example of this is a round dining table with chairs around it, or a spiral staircase. When a composition is arranged in radial balance, the central element becomes the focal point. Radial balance can provide interesting arrangements in a room and is normally achieved through repetition of form, texture and colour.

A view from the bottom of a modern spiral staircase.

Focal Point

Every room needs a focal point. This is a feature or area of a room that grabs your attention and draws your eye. In the language of interior design, having a focal point creates emphasis.

Emphasis is the design principle that deals with the dominance of an area of interest. If you want to achieve an effective, engaging design, you should aim to have a mixture of dominant and subordinate objects to draw the eye around the interior.

Interior design's biggest enemy is boredom. A well-designed room always has, depending on the size of it, one or more focal points. A focal point must be dominant to draw attention and interesting enough to encourage the viewer to look further. A focal point therefore, must have a lasting impression but must also be an integral part of the decoration linked through scale, style, colour or theme. A fireplace or a flat screen television is the first example that most people think of when we talk about a room's focal point.

If you don't have a natural focal point in your space, you can create one by highlighting a particular piece of furniture, artwork, or by simply painting a contrasting colour or putting up a striking wallpaper in one area. Try to maintain balance, though, so that the focal point doesn't grab all of the attention. A focal point makes a room feel more inviting and balanced. Without a focal point a room will feel chaotic and uninviting

If your room has a fireplace, picture window with a great view, or beautiful piece of furniture, you will want to make the most of it by making it stand out. It is easy to highlight this feature with the furniture arrangement, accessories, use of colour and light. For example you can frame the window and the view by hanging some eye-catching curtains. A fabulous fabric in a simple style will draw the eye to this focal point. Be sure the seating is arranged to highlight the view. Create a U-shaped conversation area and anchor it with a rug. You can place a large piece of furniture, such as an armoire, on the largest wall and place a pretty chair next to it.

A focal point must be dominant to draw attention and interesting enough to encourage the viewer to look further.

TOP RIGHT:
Asymmetrical balance done well can look stunning as in this flower arrangement.

A desk or console table with a large painting or mirror above it can be a focal point. Accessorise with a pair of lamps and one or two interesting objects. Paint the wall a contrasting colour for further emphasis. Create a gallery wall as your focal point. Start with some of your favorite photographs and frame them in the same style and colour.

In the bedroom the bed is the logical focal point. The easiest way to bring attention to the bed is with a headboard. If you don't have a headboard you can purchase an upholstered one in the fabric of your choice or you can hang a gorgeous fabric behind your bed. As an alternative a decorative screen behind the bed makes an interesting and elegant headboard. If you are lucky enough to have an architectural feature in your bedroom such as a fireplace or picture window, decide whether this feature or the bed will act as the main focal point and focus the attention there. Don't ignore the other feature, but one should have more prominence. The vanity unit can be the focal point in the bathroom. Use accessories and a special mirror to highlight it and choose your lighting wisely. The fixtures above the vanity unit should be functional as well as beautiful.

So what do you do if you have a lot of small items, for instance, a lot of photographs, a collection of treasured objects, or a lot of books? The trick is to treat them as one big item. Display them together rather than have them scattered around the home. As long as they all have something in common then they will have more impact if they are displayed closely together. If you have many family photographs that you want to display on the wall then arrange them so they are contained within a rectangle, not touching, but reasonably close together. If your photographs are in stand up photo frames then group them all together on one shelf and watch as everyone loves to go over and look at them. If you have some trophies that are important then plan how best to display them together.

Clever lighting can add interest to your display, shelves can be lit from the front or behind with LED ropes, sculptures can be lit from below and paintings from above, you may want lighting within your furniture or from under your furniture if they are suspended from the floor as with kitchen and bathroom cupboards. How you choose to light your accessories will certainly affect their impact in the room.

A room that has no dominant element is bland and tedious. Once you introduce a focal point and a few visual accents you create an effective design and engage the eyes in an interesting tour of the interior.

This beautiful picture is the focal point in this hallway emphasised by the hallway table placed below it.

A desk or console table with a large painting or mirror above it can be a focal point.

Rhythm

Rhythm in design, as in music, is all about creating patterns of repetition and contrast to create visual interest. Rhythm in interior design carries the eye along a path at a pace that is comfortable for the viewer. Rhythm can be found in the repetitive use of a colour, pattern, texture, line or even in furniture pieces. Using these tools will impart a sense of movement to your space, leading the eye from one design element to another.

There are five major types of rhythm:

Repetition establishes rhythm through the repetitive use of an element. It establishes a continuity and a flow of rhythm. For example, a colour repeated throughout an interior, grouping artwork to create a whole, or even a place setting can create rhythm if the eye can smoothly connect rather than jump or leap from one object to another. Too much repetition unrelieved by contrast of some sort leads to monotony and too little repetition leads to confusion.

Alternation is the sequence of two or more components by which the eye can follow a rhythmic pattern. This could be alternate coloured cushions, of alternate sized cushions, on a sofa. You may choose to have two different styled dining chairs, placed alternatively next to each other around a dining table, or smaller and larger pictures displayed on a wall in alternate sizes. This can be a great way of introducing variety without loosing order.

Progression is taking an element and increasing or decreasing one or more of its qualities. The most obvious implementation of this would be a gradation by size. A collection of vases of varying sizes on a sideboard creates interest, because of the natural progression shown. Progression can also be achieved through the order of similar artworks increasing in height along a staircase, leading the eye to the next level, or via colour, such as a monochromatic colour scheme, where each element is a slightly different shade of the same hue.

These cushions alternate with each other to create a more interesting pattern than just having two cushions.

TOP LEFT:
The layout of this, 'The backs of these chairs have a repeating pattern, which although simple makes them very attractive'.

Interior Design Secrets . . . .

Contrast is an abrupt change that forms interesting, repetitive rhythm, it is easy to achieve by putting two elements in opposition to one another, such as a white and black pillow on a bed. Opposition can also be implied by contrast in form, such as circles and squares together or through a mix of contemporary with antique, modern paintings in a traditional room, mismatching chairs at a solid table, combining busy and plain patterned fabrics and so on. Contrast helps to enliven a space and create interest and individuality, but it needs to be used according to the style and theme and with restraint, or it may lead to confusion.

Transition is a bit harder to define. It tends to be a smoother flow, where the eye naturally glides from one area to another. The most common transition is the use of a curved line to gently lead the eye, such as a spiral staircase or an arched doorway. Curved lines have become very popular in kitchen design to smoothly take the eye from the food preparation and cooking area to the kitchen table and socialising area.

Harmony

Harmony is created when all the elements act together to create an unified message. Just as rhythm can create excitement, harmony creates a sense of restfulness. For instance, you can create harmony by using just one colour, even though they vary greatly in shape, size and texture.

An interior can be compared to a jigsaw puzzle, where a variety of diverse elements – furniture, lights, flooring, wall treatments, soft furnishings and so on are combined together to form a composition. Harmony is a design principle that deals with the pleasing combination of those elements. An interior denotes harmony when all its diverse components relate to each other and to the space that contains them in an attractive, pleasing way.

While balance unifies the space through the careful arrangements of both similar and dissimilar elements, harmony relies on the selection of elements that share a common trait or characteristic like shape, colour, texture, material or pattern.

The gradual change of colour in these mosaic tiles can create a stunning effect on a wall or floor.

TOP RIGHT:
This Designer Guild's wallpaper creates a real 'wow factor' in this bedroom. The plain light coloured carpet prevents the room from looking dark with too much pattern.

This beautiful edging tile is a good example of transition rhythm.

This country cottage bedroom follows all the interior design principles with harmonious effect.

You can introduce variety in an interior in many ways.

The repetition of this common characteristic gives unity to the interior and provides visual harmony. A simple way to achieve harmony, for example, is to use a monochromatic colour scheme; another way is to use similar textures to give a unified look to the space. Don't overdo unity, though, if you use too many elements that are similar, you could end up with a coordinated interior that lacks interest, a dull and boring composition. To avoid this, you need to introduce variety, giving the eye a number of different shapes, colours, textures and details to look at. But don't add too much variety just for the sake of interest, variety carried to an extreme can result in chaos, the very opposite of harmony. You can introduce variety in an interior in many ways you could vary orientation, size, colour, detail characteristics, and texture. A great example is to have the same chair in different fabrics around a dining table, or have chairs in different style and size but all of the same material like wood. Another example is to have an array of cushions on a sofa in different coloured silks, or different shaped cushions in different fabrics but all the same colour.

You could say that harmony in interior design is the result of a careful balance between order and disorder, between unity and variety.

If you want to achieve a harmonious interior in a simple way, first you can unify the space choosing the majority of elements that share a common characteristic, then you can add a few, carefully chosen elements that have a variety of unique, individual accents that allows you to add your unique style.

Scale *refers to the overall size of objects and the space that they are in. At its simplest, this design principle says that if you have a large room, the objects within it should also be large and the converse in a small room.*

Proportion defines the relationship of the size of an object to others that surround it. So that small bedside lamps would look very odd either side of a large king sized bed for example.

Balance *is all about equalising or approximating the visual balance of objects. This can be done symmetrically, asymmetrically or in a radial arrangement. Balance is created not just through shape, but also through colour, pattern, texture and light.*

Focal point *creates a visual anchor in the room. It could be something obvious in a room like a fireplace or you may need to create one with an unusual piece of furniture, or a feature wall, whatever it is a focal point stops your room from looking boring and uninteresting.*

Rhythm *defines the repetition of patterns and contrast to create visual excitement. Its purpose is to move your eye around the room at a pace that is comfortable and flows...*

Harmony *is created when the design has a unified message. Whereas rhythm expresses excitement in a design, harmony gives a sense of restfulness, so that all the elements within the room, belong together.*

Understanding design principles

HOT TIPS

8

Adding the finishing touches

The latest may not be the greatest

This may sound obvious but it is important to make sure you are not carried away by the latest trends and create something, which quickly looks out of date and perhaps does not fit with the overall character of your home. To some extent you can't avoid some styles looking dated and it is very easy to walk into a house and take an educated guess in which decade it was last decorated. However you don't want this to happen after only a very short period of time. The average redecoration cycle is seven years and probably even longer for a kitchen or bathroom. The coloured bathroom suites, paint effects on kitchen cupboards and large spot lights are very much out of fashion, however how will we feel about the black tiles so popular at the moment in bathrooms in five years' time? So if you are investing a lot of money and don't want to be refurbishing a room for a long time then avoid making a fashion statement with a permanent fixture.

There is flow from the dining room through the small entrance lobby to the drawing room through the use of colour, style and light.

ABOVE:
This 1960's chair looks fabulous in a retro style design.

ABOVE RIGHT:
The attention to detail on this curtain heading gives it a unique and interesting effect.

The choice of accessories can transform an otherwise plain design.

The analogy with clothes fashion works here as well. Think of it as investing in an expensive little black dress and accessorising with modern and exciting things. With the dress it may be a pair of faux leopard skin court shoes with matching handbag and with a sofa it may be some leopard skin effect cushions with co-ordinating lampshades. The principles are the same. This allows you to update your scheme by changing the accent items without having to completely re-decorate, by introducing some expensive things in small quantities you can create that wow factor and make it easy to adjust the look for the seasons, especially at Christmas. It is a fine line between creating an interesting design that won't date and being so conservative that a scheme becomes bland and boring. The choice of accessories can transform an otherwise plain design. A quirky chair, unusual lamp or an odd shaped mirror, for example can add style, creativity and reflect modern trends without the design becoming a fashion victim.

Achieving the "complete design" feel for your home

At the beginning of this book we talked about how your interior design needs to reflect the personality that you want your home to have, whilst respecting its style and character. Respecting the style and character of your home is another reason not to get swayed by the latest trends. Modern colours, textures and patterns should only be introduced into the scheme if they are suitable. This becomes more difficult when the property has a distinctive age and style, like a beamed thatched cottage, an Edwardian manor house or even a New York style loft apartment. These properties have a personality and style as part of their infrastructure and this will impact your choice of design.

Remember that the house needs to feel "complete" in terms of its overall design even if the rooms aren't being decorated all at the same time. Whilst they do not need to be decorated in the same colours or use the same textures and patterns, they should have a common thread reflecting its style and personality, otherwise the house could look as if different people have decorated it and lost its identity. This doesn't mean you have to be rigidly faithful to the era in which it was built, although there are some fantastic heritage fabrics and colours that have been well researched for you to access, but that the house does need to look complete.

You may know exactly what you want in order to match the style of your house, and unfortunately that may mean that your choice of a particular colour or style can be difficult to find as it is not currently 'on trend'. You may have to do a little creative searching on the Internet to track down things with a retro feel.

Overwhelming choice and temptation

The challenge is that the availability of products will be dictated by the companies that produce them and what they deem to be fashionable. To encourage you to replace your furniture and fabrics, the interior design market wants to constantly create new trends and there are consultants who forecast colour trends, which the interior design and fashion industry use. The interior design industry follows more closely the fashion industry than ever before so that if sparkly accessories are fashionable for clothes they will also start to appear on the fabrics, furniture and lighting. You may

The interior design market wants to constantly create new trends.

The temptation on us to buy the latest trend is all around us.

have noticed that Swarovski crystals are no longer only in jewellery. They are now on chandeliers and upholstery fabrics have incorporated them. They may look wonderful but do they fit in your decoration scheme? The temptation on us to buy the latest trend is all around us.

There is also a trend for smaller manufacturers to create competitively priced items for our homes and as they are more flexible and adaptable in varying their designs they are able to respond to an ever-changing market. The Internet gives you the chance to explore a far greater range of choices and the smaller manufacturers are able to advertise products that previously you wouldn't have had the opportunity to see. Whilst the Internet is a fantastic place to review all your options, the choices are enormous and as with comments in the fabric section if you don't know what you are looking for you can be overwhelmed by the items available. So don't forget to use your mood board to establish your search criteria and keep your choices on track.

To help you with the finishing touches, I've put together some important considerations and tips for choosing curtains, flooring, walls and some of those other important things that add the extra special something to your home.

Curtain considerations

There is a lot more to think about than just whether your curtains should be long or short or whether you tie them back or not? As choice of fabric, pattern and colour, and style of curtain has an enormous impact on your interior design, there are a lot of decisions that need to be thought through, some of which you may never have realised. I would always recommend having your curtains made rather than bought from a shop. They will then be made specifically for that window, you will have a far greater choice in the finished look and they will simply look so much better. If the budget is limited, I would always recommend compromising on the quality of the fabric rather than how it is made. A good curtain maker can make very inexpensive fabric look wonderful and suggest ideas to help you. To help you plan and communicate well with your curtain maker, I have outlined below all the factors you need to think about when planning your curtains.

Length

Length is an important factor. Do you want long or short curtains? Of course the decision may be simple due to physical limitations such as a radiator below the window, or furniture that sits within the window where short curtains are the only choice, or large windows with patio doors where you would always choose full length curtains. If there is no obvious choice then long curtains give a more formal, sophisticated look fabulous in a Georgian drawing room, whereas short are a more informal, casual style great in a country cottage. Of course the longer the curtain, the more fabric you use and the more expensive your curtains will be.

Do you combine short and long in the same room or choose blinds where long curtains can't be used? This depends on the overall combination of the windows, whether they sit next to each other, whether there is symmetry in the arrangement, or whether the varying lengths will not be obvious as they disappear behind a piece of furniture. Try not to have more than two different lengths in one room or the room could look very untidy.

Try not to have more than two different lengths in one room.

Adding the finishing touches

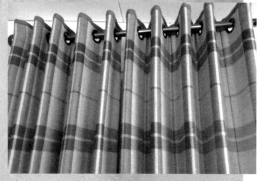

If you are going to have short curtains I would advise that they are between 5cms and 10cms below the window sill. Long curtains should clear the floor by about 1cm.

Where the windows are wide be sure to take measurements at either side of the window and in the middle, you may be surprised how much they can differ. In older properties, this can be because the top edge of the window slopes, or that the floor slopes. You don't want the curtains to make the room look crooked. If you are planning on having full length curtains and there is an obvious pattern this could be a problem. You can adjust the curtain track to be parallel with the floor or choose plain or a vertical strip fabric where the change in length wouldn't show. If your curtains are on a ceiling track with a sloping floor then consider puddling your curtains on the floor. Puddling is where the curtain length is greater than the length of the window to create a puddle of fabric on the floor. This is great for dress curtains, where they will not be drawn closed.

Headings

The choice of curtain heading is also very important as it changes completely the style and look of the window even with the same fabric. It also affects the quantity of fabric used and the cost of making them. Here are the most common headings:

Standard gather: probably the most commonly used of all the options. This is an even gather across the width of the curtain usually on a curtain tape that is pulled into a gather to fit the track. If a curtain pole is to be used then make sure that there are enough rings to stop the curtains from sagging. The amount of gather depends on the quantity of fabric used and is often used behind a pelmet where the heading can't be seen.

Double or triple pleat: this is where the gather is either two or three folds of the fabric and is pinched together into a pleat at regular intervals, usually around 10cms apart. The pleat can be decorated with a button, tassel or small rosette, for example and can lift an otherwise plain set of curtains especially if they are coordinated with tie backs. This is a smart look and would suit modern and traditional homes. A good curtain maker can hand make this curtain heading and space the pleats to match the pattern of the fabric so that the curtains look just as good open as they do closed, and to suit the dimensions of the window. You don't want to choose expensive fabric and when they are open the pattern is lost in the folds of the pleats. This style is probably the most popular handmade curtain heading.

Goblet pleat: this is very similar to the above except that the fabric in the pleat is expanded to make a goblet, usually stuffed with something to maintain its shape. This is a grander and more opulent look than the triple pleat and is more commonly used in long curtains in period properties. The goblet pleats can be linked with cord to complete the heritage look.

Eyelet heading: this is where there are holes created in the top of the fabric for the pole to be threaded through. This is probably the least expensive of all the choices as it uses the least amount of fabric and is relatively easy to make. This is a very modern look and a favourite with the young. It's a great choice for a children's bedroom where you know you will be changing the decor frequently and it needs to withstand some rough treatment.

Fixed headings: these are where a curtain is fixed to a pole, board or something and it therefore cannot be drawn back. There is usually a tie back or hold back that takes the curtain back and drapes it across the window. On these curtains any heading can be chosen including the above as they are only there for decoration. This is a great choice where you may want to obscure the window or the view and move the attention to the curtain. Puddling a curtain like this on the floor will give a rich elegant look.

Voiles and nets: these are lightweight, unlined curtains (you wouldn't need to line voile or net) that filter light and are great where strong light needs to be diffused or privacy is required without loosing too much light. The introduction of voiles has meant that fabric houses have developed a large range of styles and colours and have moved away from the conservative net curtains that used to be so popular. These can be combined with curtains or blinds. You will need a double pole in order to have curtains and voiles so that they can be operated independently. There are a lot of traditional designs available too which can further enhance the heritage feel if that is your objective. Light weight curtains should have weights in the hem to ensure they hang straight and don't kick out, this is especially important with voiles and nets.

There are a large variety of unusual curtain headings and finishes that you can choose to develop that very individual style. Wendy Baker has produced a number of curtain and blind sketch books that can give you some original ideas for window treatments. You can order them on line at **wendybakerinteriors.co.uk/ wendysbooks**

TOP:
This pretty GP & J Baker fabric with contrast lining is in a fixed position in an Italian strung style.

BOTTOM:
The border can introduce pattern as shown here.

BELOW:

A trim can add a lovely finishing touch to a fabric as it does with this Sanderson fabric.

BOTTOM:

The red border highlights the red in the pattern of this fabric creating a stronger look.

Lining

How should you line your curtains? Firstly never have unlined curtains. Lining gives the curtains, body, hanging weight and protects the main fabric. So are they to be simply lined or interlined, interlining is a thicker fabric that sits between the fabric and lining, or blackout lining, which you may choose for the bedrooms to black out light. Interlining also improves the look and hanging qualities of any fabrics but is particularly recommended for light weight fabrics such as silks. I will always recommend that my client has their curtains interlined. You can line your curtains with another fabric, which can look fabulous where the curtain is draped back to show the lining, or you could choose a coloured lining. Your curtains will then look good equally from the inside and out.

Remember however, the impact of the sun, which can bleach fabrics, even in this country, and can rot silk, you need to think about the direction of the windows, are they south facing for example, and are they protected from direct sunlight.

Overlaps and returns

Overlaps and returns are something that most people don't consider but can give the curtains that finished professional look. An overlap is simply how much of an overlap one curtain has over the other when they are drawn closed. This is an important decision especially if there is a very definite large pattern repeat, otherwise I would recommend a minimum of 5 cms. The return is the depth of the final pleat at each end of the curtain below the final hook, this will determine how close to the wall the fabric returns back. This is significant if the curtains are viewed from the side especially when entering a room and if the pole or track has a large bracket and therefore curtains hang quite a way from the wall, or the curtains are on a ceiling track. A good curtain maker will give you advice on all these points.

Trimmings and borders

Trimmings and borders, these are purely decorative but can really add that personal touch to your curtains. They can also transform otherwise plain curtains and introduce a different colour, texture and pattern. You can add feathers, shells, crystals as well as the normal braids, fringes and bobbles, they come in an enormous range of colours and sizes and many fabric houses produce coordinating ranges with their fabrics. Adding borders to plain curtains can change the feel and look of any curtain and can give you an opportunity to add the accent fabric to somewhere else in the room. It just takes a little bit of courage but will be worth it.

Pelmets and valances

Pelmets and valances have made a comeback after the predominance of poles. They are a great way of disguising ugly curtain tracks, unattractive windows and can change the visual proportions of curtains and windows. It is also an opportunity to introduce a complementary fabric, a defining border or a particular style statement. They can be flat, gathered or have one of the above headings. They can also have trimmings, such as fringes and can help create a period style in your home. Pelmets can be over the top at small windows.

Tiebacks and holdbacks

Tie backs and hold backs help keep curtains in order and out of the way. They are also another way of introducing another design element. The tie backs can be made of fabric to match or co-ordinate with the curtains, or they can be made from rope with a vast range of different fringes hanging from them. There are all kinds of fringe sizes as well as bobbles, crystals, feathers and ribbons that are very beautiful and look particularly good on plain or simple patterned curtains. Hold backs are a large disc attached to the wall by a bracket which the curtains are tucked to one side. Hold backs can come in any design from plain wood to glass or resin which is made to look like something else. You can have them to match your finials or any plaster work such as a ceiling rose or elaborate cornice. They are best with long curtains where there is enough quantity of fabric to look right with this type of gathering in the curtain.

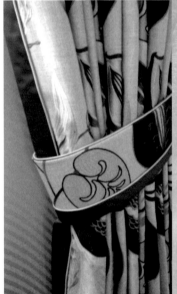

LEFT:
Co-ordinating tie backs can be designed to compliment beautiful curtains.

BELOW:
Holdbacks are available in many different designs and materials that match the curtain pole and finials.

ABOVE:
A heritage style pole and finial co-ordinate beautifully with the fabric.

RIGHT:
A traditional pole reflects the style of this room.

Finials can really add a style statement to your pole and curtains.

Poles, brackets and finials

Poles, brackets and finials now come in an enormous variety of colours and finishes to suit your interior design scheme. The size of the pole should be in proportion with the visual weight of the curtains and be able to take the weight. It may mean you will need more brackets and your supplier will be able to advise you depending on the size of the window, the type of fabric in the curtains as well as your choice of lining. Finials can really add a style statement to your pole and curtains, make sure there is sufficient room either side of the pole and above if it is close to the ceiling for your chosen design. There are suppliers that will make finials to your specification and can co-ordinate them with your fabric, an example of such a company is Bryony Alexander the web address is **bryonyalexander.com**

Blinds

What if you don't want curtains, or there just isn't room, or the conditions don't allow you to have folds of fabric at the window. The obvious alternative is blinds. Like curtains blinds have a variety of styles. The blind can sit within the window recess, which is neat and tidy and is very useful where space is at a premium. It does however reduce light, and you are unable to put anything on the window sill. They can sit outside the window, which takes up more space but gives you the flexibility to use different styles.

Roller blinds are probably the most common type of blind. They come in a huge range of colours and fabric styles, they can fit any window and work well in bathrooms and at VELUX windows. They can be operated by a remote or timer and are within most budgets. However they are not very exciting when open.

Venetian blinds are horizontal slats that now come in any colour and material including wood. They not only block out light but can filter it too. They are a very modern and unfussy style which suits a minimalist look. Vertical blinds are where the slats are vertical and very popular in offices. There are vertical screens which are much wider slats that usually hang from the ceiling and they stack to one side, one in front of another, each screen can be in a different fabric or different colour and can be a funky alternative to traditional curtains and blinds.

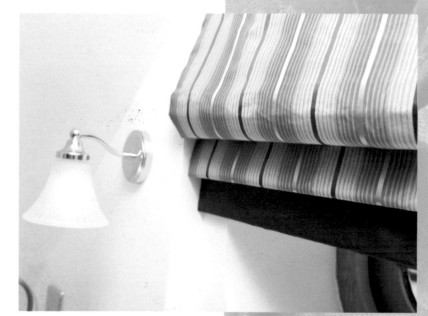

TOP:
This elegant roman blind adds colour and pattern to this bathroom.

BOTTOM:
The choice of venetian blinds here is both practical and stylish.

Roman blinds are folds of fabric that when lifted create a pelmet effect and gives you the opportunity to have a beautifully expensive fabric that may be impractical for curtains. These can look great with dress curtains to develop an elaborate co-ordinated window treatment.

Austrian and London blinds are elaborate and can dress a window with fabric when curtains are not a practical alternative but a pretty dressing is desired. They look best half open which shows the fabric and the shape of the blind at its best.

Blinds can have borders and trimmings just like curtains, especially across the bottom of the blind where they will be seen. The bottom of the blind does not have to be straight and can be a variety shapes such as scallops or zigzag, there is no limit to what shape, however if there is a pattern to the fabric this needs to be taken into consideration.

Lambrequins are not very common but they have a pelmet that not only sits across the top of the window but to both sides as well and sometimes a simple blind operates behind it. It is an alternative way of dressing a window and as with curtain pelmets there is an opportunity to introduce a contrasting fabric. They work best at very large windows where a blind on its own looks a bit feeble.

TOP:
Striped fabric works particularly well as a roman blind.

BOTTOM:
Although this style is out of fashion at the moment it is a pretty way to dress a window.

Alternatives to fabric

Shutters have become very popular and can look equally great in a country cottage as well as a modern town house. They can be decorative on the outside or inside of the window, come in almost any colour, be full or half window and can be used in conjunction with other window treatments. They can be covered in fabric, have double or triple fold so that they don't stick out too far when folded back, and even just operate on the lower half of the window. Where there are slats within the shutter they can be moved to allow a degree of light in, they can also work well in bathrooms and kitchens where fabric may not be suitable.

Stained glass is another way of giving privacy to a room without losing light. It can be a beautiful way of introducing a new unique design to your space. It can be inserted in a door panel, window pane, front door and it is possible to have your stained glass designed for you and can introduce a highly personalised style statement. They can look fabulous in a window overlooking the stairs, or a bathroom window that is visible from the front of the house, or even an internal window in an older property.

*Shutters can
be decorative
on the outside
or inside of the
window.*

Adding the finishing touches

Flooring

Floors are the hardest working surfaces in your home. They are expected to cope with the pounding of innumerable footsteps, plus take the drops and spills of everyday life. Not only do they work hard, but we want them to look good too, after all floors can make the difference between a dull and an exciting room. Floors are tricky and expensive to install so you need to plan well.

Considerations

The choice is so wide today that you can go beyond simple practicality in your choices and find flooring to suit the house, the individual and your lifestyle. You need to choose materials that are compatible with your house and design scheme.

The design and creative use of resilient flooring works well in open plan spaces.

An English country style home would suit stone or wooden floors, a house from the Victorian era would look best with fitted traditionally designed carpets, parquet flooring or quarry tiles, an Arts and Crafts home could have wooden floors with intricate inlays and scattered rugs, whereas a contemporary look may feature, exotic woods, natural stone, or ultra modern materials such as rubber or terrazzo. The demands of a room are very important when selecting the right type of flooring, you wouldn't put a shaggy carpet in a bathroom for example. Durability in certain areas such as hallways is key and some materials, such as lesser quality carpets won't be able to cope.

Safety is another important factor especially if you have family members that have mobility problems, also in certain rooms such as bathrooms which need a non slip floor.

There are other considerations, for instance where there are small children or allergy sufferers or even pets, cleanliness may be paramount.

Budget is also a key element. There is an enormous variation between say, a marble or leather floor and the least expensive vinyl or synthetic carpet. If your pockets aren't deep enough there are some great imitations around. Remember to allow for installation costs as well as materials.

The type of material, colour and pattern of your floor can affect the look of a room just as in any other area of design. Small rooms call for small patterns, such as parquet flooring, while larger rooms have space for bigger shapes, like stone slabs. Dark floors define space well, while pale or neutral tones deflects attention elsewhere, making the room seem bigger. Carpets and matte finishes absorb light confining the scale of a room, while shiny surfaces create a brighter, airier look. So whilst a wooden floor may be dark this can be counterbalanced with a polished surface, or a light carpet with a textured surface will not look so bright. Remember to consider how adjacent rooms work together, they should be in harmony, so the transition between different parts of the house doesn't jar.

Stone floors

Stone is an excellent flooring material because it is beautiful and durable. It takes the wear and tear of everyday life and improves with age. Stone is also versatile. There is such an incredible assortment of colours, patterns and textures that, if your budget allows, it will complement any room.

The disadvantage is that they feel cool, anything dropped on it will most likely break and it can be very unforgiving on the feet. However you can use underfloor heating to warm the surface and there is a type of stone that will suit any interior decorating style.

The main types of stone floors are marble, granite, limestone and sandstone. All stone requires a strong sub-floor that can bear the weight.

Hard Flooring

Examples of this type of flooring are tiles, bricks, concrete, glass and metal. They have the same advantages and disadvantages as stone floors, however they are often a cheaper alternative. The most common are tiles and bricks which means they are laid in a pattern. Choosing the pattern can be as important as selecting the colour, since this can have a major impact on the mood of a room and how the eye

Stone takes the wear and tear of everyday life and improves with age.

Adding the finishing touches

is drawn. An overly complicated design makes the room seem cluttered, but a rigidly regular pattern can look uniform and boring, so planning is crucial.

To create a truly modern look you may wish to choose concrete which can come in an amazing array of colours and effects; glass, which can also be coloured, opaque or indeed lit; or metal, which can come in tiles or sheets, and may be recycled so is environmentally friendly and can be treated to look like brass, bronze, copper and other metals even though it is made from galvanised steel. As with stone floors they don't absorb sound so not ideal in quiet areas where there are a lot of people.

Wooden Flooring

Wood has long been a favourite flooring choice, and for several reasons. Wood is beautiful, adding warmth and a unique style to your home as no two wooden floors will look the same. Wood offers the same performance and style of stone flooring at a more affordable price. Well-sourced wood is environmentally responsible and less costly floors have been developed such as pre-finished, engineered and glueless varieties.

Engineered floors have a veneer of beautiful expensive wood, whilst the

The natural tones of stone can look good anywhere.

bottom layer is usually plywood, and they provide the same look, but they can't be sanded and refinished as you would for a complete wooden floor.

Wood enhances almost any decorative scheme, the heavy grain of hardwoods such as oak, is great for a country look, but for a more contemporary style try using a lighter wood such as pale beech. Wood is not suitable in wet areas such as kitchens and bathrooms, however as a solid floor it is warmer and more forgiving than stone and hard floors.

Resilient flooring

A resilient floor, for example vinyl, is hard working, but largely ignored or viewed with disdain as the cheap option. However it is easy to install and maintain and it offers comfort and value. Although vinyl is the most common choice, there is linoleum, rubber, cork and leather, which are gaining popularity because of their environmental benefits. As well as being made from natural materials, linoleum has the added advantage of being non-allergenic. Resilient means this type of flooring springs back into shape if it gets dented, one of its most useful characteristics. It is comfortable to walk on, comes in colours, designs and effects to suit any budget and can mimic the appearance of other materials well. They are easy to clean and resistant to scuffs, but the softer material does mean they are susceptible to scratches, dents and burns. This type of flooring does have a limited life depending on the thickness of the material.

Soft flooring

Carpet is the obvious example of a soft floor and the most popular. It is soft and warm underfoot and offers beautiful colours and patterns, creating a focal point in a room. Carpet brings a soothing intimacy to homes, and no other material matches the luxurious feel of cushioned wool under bare feet.

Carpet will provide insulation, absorbs sound and is slip resistant, but it can't cope with moisture and is more difficult to clean. Heavy furniture will dent a carpet, which isn't a problem until you want to rearrange the room.

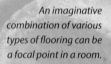

An imaginative combination of various types of flooring can be a focal point in a room.

Rugs bring warmth to stone and protect a wooden floor from dirt and scratches.

With carpets more than any other flooring material, you get what you pay for. They come in different grades of suitability, fibres and density of fibre, which is measured by the quantity of tufts per square inch. Natural fibres such as sisal, jute, coir and seagrass are alternatives to the traditional wool and synthetic fibres which produce a hard wearing, stain resistant floor covering that is ecologically friendly and becoming increasingly popular. They usually come in neutral colours and rich textures, but they tend to be more prickly and less durable than traditional carpets.

There are many terms to describe a variety of carpets, an Axminster derives its name from the loom on which it is woven, the pile is inserted into the weave from above allowing for many colours and patterns, it can be pure wool or a wool and fibre mix, cut pile, shaggy or contoured. The Wilton also derives its name from the type of loom it is woven on but because the loom weaves the yarn in a continuous strand it means only a limited number of colours can be used. The pile is close textured which produces a smooth velvety effect. Axminsters and Wiltons use labour intensive processes and consequently they are expensive, tufted carpets are much quicker to produce and therefore less expensive. They are made by inserting tufts into a pre-woven backing and they are anchored there by latex. The pile can be cut, looped or twisted. A cord carpet is woven from a mixture of yarns containing some cow, calf or goat hair and it looks rather like corduroy.

Rugs offer a halfway house between soft and hard floors. Rugs bring warmth to stone, protect a wooden floor from dirt and scratches, lessen noise and bring comfort to a tiled surface. They can transform a room by adding colour texture and pattern and come in an amazing array of designs, from traditional to contemporary, indeed you can design your own rug.

Floors do a tough job and they need to be well maintained in order to help them stay beautiful and effective for as long as possible. Consider how much time, effort and money you are prepared to invest in this before you finalise your choice. Hard floors will need to be swept and washed regularly and soft floors will need vacuuming and occasional professional cleaning. Identify the high traffic areas in your home and where comfort is your priority, and plan the flooring accordingly. Choose the highest quality you can afford as choosing a cheap flooring material does not always save you money in the long-term.

Interior Design Secrets . . . .

Wall Treatments

There are so many ways in which to decorate a wall that this subject could be a book in itself. Here we will summarise most of the options, some of which are easy to do yourself and others, which will certainly need professional application.

Painted finishes

The simplest way in which to decorate your wall is to apply emulsion paint. It is relatively easy to do, inexpensive, easy to maintain and clean, and you can simply update your décor whenever you feel like it. Emulsion paints are water based so they are safe to use anywhere. There is an enormous range of colours available, especially with the main brands giving you the option of having your paint mixed to order, previously only available to the trade.

Emulsion paints are water based so they are safe to use anywhere.

This dark grey accent wall in a teenage boys bedroom creates a modern smart room.

It's best you practise specialist painting techniques on paper before starting on the walls.

A simply painted wall may well be the back-drop to other paint techniques and wall treatments or complement a focal wall of wallpaper for example. If you are emulsioning your walls white or a pale neutral colour, you will need to apply at least three coats to give depth and richness to the finish otherwise it can look pale and wishy washy. If you are painting a strong colour over an existing strong colour you are advised to cover the wall in white emulsion first so that the original colour does not bleed through and affect the new one. If you are only going to paint your walls then preparing the surface is important as any imperfections will show.

Decorative paint finishes

Whilst painting a wall a flat colour is easy it can sometimes look rather bland and there are many paint techniques that can make them look exciting. The techniques of sponging, rag rolling, stippling and dragging, so popular in the 1980s and 1990s have declined in popularity but still can be a great way of decorating a wall without going to the expense of wallpaper. There is an art to it, and I would recommend you practise your chosen technique on paper before starting on the walls and because most of them involve diluting paint with glazes make sure you give yourself enough time to complete a wall in one go.

There are simpler techniques such as painting stripes, horizontally or vertically either in two colours, two shades of the same colour or even a mix of matt and gloss of the same colour. Vertical stripes will make the walls seem higher and lift the ceiling visually, whilst horizontal stripes will make the room seem wider.

You can repeat simple shapes in a contrasting colour, such as circles, you can use stencils to paint shapes like flowers or columns, in fact you can buy stencils that allow you to create your own mural. Great if you have a good imagination but your drawing skills aren't as good as you would like. Even better for rooms such as childrens' bedrooms and playrooms where you can create something that they would love.

If stenciling seems too much like hard work then there is now a large range of wall stickers available on the Internet. Examples of these are **mywallstickers.co.uk** and **allposters.co.uk.**

There are the more traditional paint techniques that have existed for years, whitewashing and distemper. They are particularly useful on rough walls. The base of whitewash is usually quicklime, which is made from limestone or chalk, mixed with water and grease or tallow to bind the water and quicklime together. As the whitewash ages a carbonisation process occurs which hardens the coating and gives it a longer life. There can be problems when it comes to redecorating. Original distempers were made of whiting bound with glue, which was then tinted with pigments such as ochre and similar earth colours to give soft chalky shades. Distemper is not often used now and is difficult to remove, but can be found on the walls and ceilings of old houses. It is possible to create the same paint finish with modern paints thus avoiding many of the problems of these paint techniques.

The ultimate in painting a wall is to create a mural. This allows you to create something unique and special to you, however you do need a great deal of artistic talent. There are professionals who can create anything you like with paint and other materials with breathtaking results. They can use paint to imitate almost any surface you would like on your walls, but is either too expensive or just not practical. A wall can be made to look like stone, marble, or wood for example. The technique of trompe l'oeil, is where paint is used to create 3D images on the wall such as, books, panelling or even a false door or cupboard. These professional artists are used a lot by interior designers to create a desired look and you may well have visited a restaurant or hotel unaware that the columns are not made of marble, or that the walls are wood paneled, they have just been painted to look like that.

The ultimate in painting a wall is to create a mural.

Surfaces can be painted to imitate any other material.

Wallpapers

The earliest recorded example of European wallpaper is said to date back to the reign of Henry VIII, but it was not until 1692 that the first wallpaper patent was issued. These early wallpapers would have been printed by hand using carved blocks of wood. There is still a demand for hand printed wallpapers produced by the old methods, but it is now more usual to print them by using a silk screen. The strength of hand printed wallpapers lies in the traditional designs, created by such notable people as William Morris, famous for his Arts and Crafts designs and Augustus Pugin best known as architect for the Houses of Parliament in London. Those who are prepared to pay the price will have wallpaper printed on high quality paper, of excellent design, coloured to individual specification, and produced by skilled craftsmen. These wallpapers can be difficult to pattern match and are probably best left for a professional decorator to hang.

This fabulous textured wallpaper from Thibaut makes a real statement.

There is a multitude of machine printed wallpapers, to suit any budget and any taste. As wallpaper has gained favour so the choice available has expanded, especially in the more elaborate designs. The quality of the wallpaper varies greatly and you certainly get what you pay for. Inexpensive papers are often difficult to hang because they are usually thin and when wet, can overstretch and dry out unevenly, or tear and therefore increase the wastage. It is not only the design of the wallpaper, which you need to consider, but also the type of paper where there are practical considerations.

Papers, which are described as washable, have been coated with a thin transparent plastic film and can be washed with soapy water, but they will not tolerate detergents or being scrubbed with abrasives. Unlike vinyls, which have a distinct and not particularly attractive plastic appearance, washable wallpapers are available in a range of finishes from matt to glossy. Vinyls are tough and waterproof and can withstand scrubbing with detergents and wear extremely well. Anti fungal wall paste should be used for hanging as the drying out process can take a long time. Vinyls react badly to fumes such as gas fires or smoke as the PVC coating discolours and that cannot be washed away.

There are two other distinctive wallpapers, Lincrusta and Anaglypta. Anaglypta has come a long way since its early days and limited choice of patterns. Some of the embossed designs resemble plaster mouldings and are very popular providing texture below a dado rail. They are useful in heavy traffic areas such as hallways where they give the warmth of wallpaper but have the practical benefits of paint. Lincrusta is more rigid than Anaglypta and is made from paper mixed with a pliable filling and linseed oil. Whilst still soft this is pressed into various textures, relief patterns and other effects, which can resemble anything from wall panelling to tiles. Both these wallpapers are useful for disguising rough and uneven walls and are usually applied in their off-white state before being painted.

ABOVE:
There are an enormous variety of wallpapers for you to choose from.

Lining papers are used to improve uneven or cracked walls before applying paint or wallpaper. It is essential under delicate wallpapers and recommended under expensive wallpapers to produce a first class finish. Lining paper can also cover up dark walls, which might grin through wallpaper. Lining papers come in different weights depending on the state of the walls and they are hung horizontally behind wallpaper so that there are no vertical joins lying directly on top of each other.

BELOW:
Reflective effects in wallpaper have become very popular and help amplify light.

There are wallpapers that imitate fabric. Flock wallpapers have become popular and the raised pile has a cut velvet appearance that gives a sense of richness that looks stunning in the right setting. They are not great in high traffic areas where a lot of fingers will mark the walls, such as hallways and they are not generally suitable for curved features like arches. There are other fabric finishes that have been the inspiration for wallpaper design such as silk, leather, cork, cane and various wood grains, just make sure that they are good quality otherwise a poor imitation can look worse than having a simply painted wall. More recently metallic papers have become fashionable and they are great in areas where light may be an issue. Instead of wallpaper, walls can be covered in maps, music score or advertising posters all directly applied to the wall to create an individual wall treatment. This works particularly well in a small room such as a downstairs cloakroom or study.

Fabric

Fabric is another very effective wall treatment, which will not only disguise poor walls but also lift them into the realms of luxury. This can be expensive but it is possible to create quite stunning effects with inexpensive cottons. The important thing to remember is that the material should always be made from natural fibres such as cotton, linen or wool as synthetic fabrics will stretch and sag according to the moisture content of the room.

There are three basic methods of walling with fabric: fabric wrapped around panels individually battened to the wall; fabric stapled directly to battens already fixed to the wall, and a track system, which totally conceals the fabric fixings. The fabric can be stretched, pleated, gathered or hung in dramatic swags depending on the look you would like to create. To complete a sumptuous effect you could also tent the ceiling, which is more difficult to do but shouldn't be dismissed. There are stretched fabric panels available on the Internet with interesting designs or you can send in your own design to create that unique style. There are a number of websites such as **edwardrayinternational.co.uk**, which you can order from.

Fabric screens, although not directly attached to a wall can be used to discreetly cover something unsightly or awkward and be a thing of beauty in its own right. Tapestries and rugs hung on a wall can look fabulous in any setting and can be a great way to decorate an otherwise difficult room such as a wall with many beams, or rough plaster, or a wall of natural materials such as stone or brick.

A tented ceiling would certainly create a 'wow' factor.

Tiles

These are traditionally used in bathrooms and kitchens for their waterproofing effect, but of course they can be used anywhere and in the Mediterranean countries they are used as decorative features both inside and outside the house where their cooling qualities are very much appreciated.

As mentioned with floor tiles it is not only the colour of the tile that is important but also its size and the configuration of the pattern. When planning on where to put the tiles don't just stop at the wet areas, think about the room as a whole so that use of tiles looks part of an integrated design rather than a break in the wall treatment because that particular area might get wet.

Tiles can be applied to half way up the wall, which in a bathroom especially, gives you the opportunity to introduce alternative textures and colours. Mirrored tiles are a very modern alternative to the traditional ceramic, porcelain or mosaic tiles. They will show up splash marks but if they are antiqued this is less of a problem and will give any room a 'wow' factor.

Tiled surfaces in a bathroom allows you to introduce pattern and colour in an otherwise plain environment.

This is a traditional wood panelling effect that creates a warm and cosy feel.

Wall panelling

Wall panelling has traditionally been wood oak panels in a period home, which has a masculine old-fashioned feel. It can be expensive and it needs a high level of skill to install. However with a clever modern design it can transform a room in more ways than with paint or wallpaper alone.

Good wall panelling becomes part of the structure of a house, it is timeless and may add value to a property so long as it is done properly. It can cover a multitude of sins and also be a useful way in which to link rooms visually. Panelling far from making a room look smaller, can give a space form and depth in an exciting way.

Wall panelling does not have to be made from wood, it can be stretched fabric as mentioned above, leather, glass or mirror. The panelling does not need to be solid pieces of wood, creative use of fretwork against a wall or mirror can give a striking result. As with tiles, the panelling may only occupy the lower half of the wall, with wallpaper or paint above.

When planning to panel a room getting the spaces in between the panels right is as important as the size of the panels themselves. This look is all about symmetry. Anyone can create the look of a classically panelled wall using MDF, some creative know how and a heritage paint colour. It is important to plan the panels on the walls on paper before you start as it is difficult to correct and will ruin your design if it is not installed properly.

Traditional tongue and groove or beaded boards can be used instead of panels and gives a room a less formal look. It looks great in a traditional bathroom where tiles can't always create the right ambience and it is flexible enough to cover pipes that can't be put in the walls or under the floor, whilst still maintaining access. In a small room this wall treatment can give feeling of a small cabin, cosy and intimate.

Anyone can create the look of a classically panelled wall using MDF.

Interior Design Secrets . . . .

They can be painted to co-ordinate with your interior design scheme. If you have inherited a tongue and groove shell with your home, when stripped of layers of paint the original wood can be sanded and waxed to a beautiful natural finish.

Brick and Stone

If you have an older property you may have found stone or bricks beneath crumbling plaster, in which case all you may need to do is clean them, treat them with a clear sealer and allow the beauty of the natural materials to shine through. Your house may be of an age where the fabric of the wall is wattle and daub, in which case you may wish to frame a portion of it and cover it with protective glass as a unique statement about your property. Some people find old clay pipes, money and newspapers that can make an interesting collection of articles that tells of the history of your home.

Brick and stone fascia can be added to the walls internally, although this isn't as popular as it was in the 1960s. This is a very dominant feature and generally has a busy pattern, texture and colour so it is important that this doesn't compete with anything else in the room. It is also difficult to remove once it is installed so be sure you have a clear idea of how it will sit within your interior design. Marble can also be added to the walls as panels or replace tiling in a bathroom. It is a beautiful material, but it is expensive and not suitable if condensation is a problem.

Other decorative wall features

Architectural features can be added to walls to give grandeur to a room, help with perspective and give a period feel. Skirting boards not only disguise the join between the wall and the floor but they can also be a decorative feature. The higher the walls the deeper the skirting board should be. The same applies to coving which can be handcrafted and designed to look like anything.

Brick and stone fascia can be added to the walls internally.

This original brick floor was a dominant feature of this room.

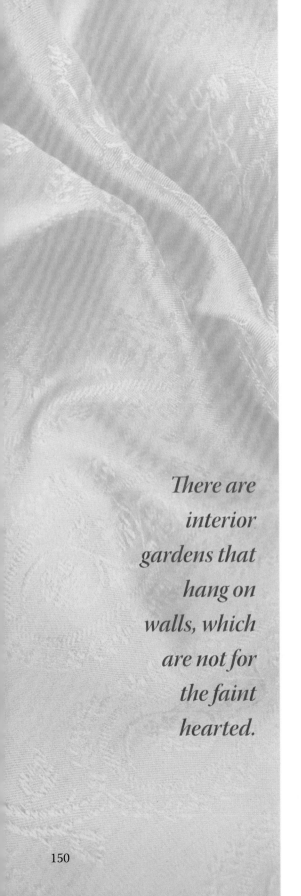

There are interior gardens that hang on walls, which are not for the faint hearted.

Dado rails and picture rails are great ways in sectioning the walls that are very high and each section being decorated in a different way. There may be painted wood panelling at the base, wallpaper in the middle and paint at the top. This was very common in some stately homes where the rooms are vast. If you are unsure where to place a dado rail or picture rail then you need to think in thirds. A dado rail should be a third of the way up from the floor and a picture rail a third of the way down from the ceiling. Even if you decide to have only one of these the same proportions should apply. A dado rail should not be half way up the wall!

Other architectural features such as columns, pedestals, and beams are a bold and imaginative way in which to decorate your room but they still need to be in keeping with the style and character of your home.

Shelving is another way to decorate a wall, either with just a small shelf and a bust or sculpture on it, you may have shelves in an alcove only or you may decide to fill the wall with shelves and display your books and other treasured objects. This all needs to be thought through as part of your design as a book-lined wall is a bold feature.

Lights can also decorate a wall with magnificent wall sconces, simple lights that wash the wall in any direction or with the popular use of LED lights they can be embedded in the wall and change colour at the press of a button on your tablet computer!

There are interior gardens that hang on walls, which are not for the faint hearted, that allow you to bring all the benefits of an outdoor garden inside. They are becoming increasingly popular in hotels and shopping centres to promote an aura of tranquility. These need to be installed by a professional who can advise you on all that you need to consider before installing one. Take a look at **urbangardensweb. com** for some ideas and inspiration.

Of course furniture against a wall in a way decorates the wall space and with the help of your mood board you will be able to see how these important elements work together. Although you don't want the furniture standing to attention around the room, you will find that an intimate grouping of furniture, artwork and lighting can help define spaces and break up the appearance of a long wall. As with everything we have discussed in this book, walls are a part of a whole scheme, albeit a very important part.

Interior Design Secrets . . . .

Finishing touches

There are so many examples of how to include something in your design that is unique, bespoke and which could transform your home from looking good to looking great. If you have ever seen something that has taken your breath away in someone else's home or in a bar, restaurant or hotel then why not re-create that impact for yourself. You may need to scale it down or even better, put your own interpretation on it. The Internet is fantastic for sourcing unusual items and if you can't find anything suitable I am sure you will be able to find someone via social media who will be able to give you advice and point you in the right direction.

Mirrors

Mirrors are not only practical but they are also wonderful aids to the interior designer. They can be both decorative and create space through deception. Entire walls can be mirrored as mentioned above, and this will double the apparent length or width of a room. Always place a mirror so that it reflects something interesting. When they are placed opposite a window the garden comes inside, or opposite a painting so that it can be appreciated from a different angle. Mirrors that are opposite each other can give an impression of infinity in the reflections although it not thought of as good feng shui.

A table can be put up against a mirror to give the impression of a much larger table. Mirrors can provide a backdrop to plants or books to create an extravagant display and with glass shelves a mirror allows ornaments to be seen from all sides. The mirror itself can be a beautiful piece with an elaborate frame, or an interesting shape. The mirror can be antiqued to give an aged effect for an old property, or you can buy an original that has antiqued naturally and wonder who before you has gazed in it at themselves.

This beautiful rug is the centre piece for this space in a large room.

Rugs and screens

Wonderful decorative effects can be achieved by using rugs and screens. Rugs can enliven floorboards and fitted carpets and define a seating area or dining area. They can also look great hung on walls. They will certainly add focus and excitement to neutral colours, indeed a rug may provide the inspiration for you to create a truly unique colour scheme.

When rugs were first imported to this country they were too valuable for people to walk on so they were displayed on large pieces of furniture such as settles and tables or draped across the back of sofas, and in the right setting this is still an elegant way of displaying them.

Kilims are a particular type of rug that is flat tapestry-woven produced from the Balkans to Pakistan. Kilims can be purely decorative or can function as prayer rugs. Modern kilims are very popular and can easily be bought on the High Street in this country.

Rugs, like carpets, can be made from a variety of fibres and this will be reflected in the price, therefore a rug made from silk will be a lot more expensive than one made purely from man-made fibres. For a hardwearing rug, wool and silk needs to be blended with other materials. There are companies that sell a variety of rug designs in a variety of sizes where you can select your colour palette for example at Jacaranda Carpets, **jacarandacarpets.com**. There are other companies where you can design your own particular rug from the size through to the colour and pattern to create something truly unique.

Screens too are wonderfully versatile. They can literally screen off part of a room, perhaps a washbasin in a bedroom, or an eating area in a living room, or they can hide objects, such as an ugly radiator, a meter or exposed pipework, which does not enhance the room. They can be purely decorative, use small ones in an empty fireplace, or tall ones as a headboard. They can be decorated with fabric or paint or even the use of decoupage to provide an instant period feel.

Plants and Flowers

A display of flowers or a collection of houseplants can be one of the most economical ways of bringing life and colour to a room. So long as a plant is chosen and situated with regard to its natural growing conditions it should thrive and last for a long time. Plants can be arranged individually or grouped together for dramatic effect, for instance in a conservatory, a large floor level plant can be enhanced by having others grouped around the base with the whole arrangement being lit by an uplighter at night. Indoor gardens hung from a wall have already been discussed in the wall treatments section. Unusual containers such as soup tureens, gravy boats and teapots can be used for flowering plants to give a quirky casual look.

Plants can be used to draw the eye from one area to another, for instance next to a window so that the division between a room and garden becomes blurred. Some plants seem to lend themselves particularly well to certain styles, for example the sharp angular shape of a palm tree would compliment an Art Deco style.

Plants can be used to draw the eye from one area to another.

LEFT:

Orchids are beautiful and can last for months.

BELOW:

Plants not only introduce colour but texture and shapes as well.

Flowers are a great way in which to celebrate the changing seasons.

These cupboard handles were chosen to co-ordinate with the bedroom's black and white colour scheme.

Fresh flowers always look good and they also can be selected to suit a particular style. Wild flowers in big jugs look wonderful in a country setting, whilst a few dramatic orchids may be the only accent needed in a smart modern loft conversion. If you don't feel confident in arranging a bouquet of flowers, select the same flower and display them in a tight bunch to create an amazing show. I especially like lilies and sunflowers displayed in this way. Once the flowers have died don't leave them in the room, dead flowers are worse than no flowers at all. Flowers are a great way in which to celebrate the changing seasons, such as daffodils and tulips, which herald the end of winter.

Dried flowers have fallen out of favour but in the right environment they still look great. The country style especially benefits from this type of flower. They can be hung in large bunches from ceiling clothes airers or meat hooks and they can be twined around willow garlands of any shape. Dried flower heads can be mixed with herbs and aromatic oils to create a pot pourri, giving a subtle fragrance to suit any occasion.

Other little details

Small details can make a tremendous difference such as the correct choice of door furniture, light switches, sockets, window latches and hinges. Radiators, that are plain and boring, can have covers, painted MDF or wooden with metal grilles, you can order flat packs on the Internet and install them yourself. Aquariums have come a long way from the traditional lone goldfish in a bowl and can now be integrated into beautiful pieces of furniture and designed to suit your style and taste. A carefully designed window seat in attractive fabric in a bay window shows that the room has been carefully considered right down to the last detail. The English have traditionally viewed blandness with horror and it is this attention to detail that can make all the difference.

The art of displaying things

The mere fact that you have taken the time to collect certain items shows their strong appeal, and grouping similar objects together makes any collection more exciting. Objects work best when they share the same trait, for instance if they are made from the same material like glass, if they are the same shape for example round, or they perform the same function such as vases, paperweights or plates. They may have the same ethnic background, they may be Aboriginal or African art, they may be tools from a craft or industry, they may track the history of a design as with tools, or they may just be objects of curiosity such as items found under the floorboards of an old house. Just about anything benefits from being grouped together, for example a group of small cameo pictures displayed together have a far greater impact than if they were displayed solo. The same goes for photographs, where a large group of family photographs grouped together looks less cluttered than if they were scattered around the house.

Objects don't have to be displayed side by side, they can be stacked such as books or hats, they can be hung from the ceiling or wall as with pots, pans and copper jelly moulds, the important thing to remember is that you need to achieve a certain balance in the way in which they are displayed, the attention to detail marks the difference between a collection and a clutter. A display of candles, crystals and other natural materials such as driftwood, can give a casual or even carefree air to a well thought through arrangement, whereas clocks, figurines and trophies require a more structured organisation.

> *It is often a case of making something ordinary look extraordinary.*

Traditional games such as chess, items like musical instruments and sports memorabilia were once hidden in cupboards or attics but are now seen as objects of interest thanks to pubs and restaurants that have shown how such things can make a fantastic display. It is often a case of making something ordinary look extraordinary in the way it is displayed, such as a stylish dress hung on the back of a door in a bedroom, a pretty hat nonchalantly hung on the corner of a free standing mirror, or an attractive piece of lace draped over the back of a chair. It must mean something to you and look at home as part of your interior design scheme.

You want to achieve, in the seemingly effortlessness way that you put things together, the balance between "just enough" and "too much", and between "careful planning" and "enjoyable accidents".

The ingredients of the best English rooms are a bit like the best food. Sometimes it is good to keep it simple and light and at other times richness and flamboyant detail have their part to play. However the most magical and sometimes elusive part of English decoration is gentle, slow and roasted over time.

Interior Design Secrets . . . .

A word about Feng Shui

Many of you will have heard of **Feng Shui**, but you may be unsure how it relates to interior design. There are **Feng Shui** interior design consultants who can give you specific advice about your home, so here I have outlined a few of the basic principles.

- *Feng Shui is the art and science of organising space to maximise positive energy. It originated in ancient China and recently has become very popular in the western world.*

- *Feng Shui tells us that positive energy enters the house through the front door, so the front of the house should be welcoming and tidy, with no clutter or obstacles. Remove dead plants and broken items as they will block the energy entering.*

- *Decluttering every room is absolutely essential to promoting a harmonious home and life. Clutter in the home restricts the flow of positive energy and can result in cluttered thinking. Tidiness promotes feelings of tranquility and anything that is broken, unused or brings back unhappy memories should be thrown away.*

- *Furniture needs to be positioned so as not to restrict free passage through the room and you should sit with your back to the wall wherever possible. This will allow energy to flow through from one room to another.*

- *Work or home offices should be kept very distinct from living or sleeping areas. Where they are mixed relaxation is difficult and if you work in your bedroom it may prevent you getting a good night's sleep.*

- *Repairs to your home should be made as quickly as possible to enable energy to flow freely.*

- *Mirrors are believed to reflect positive energy, therefore doubling its potency and they prevent the flow of negative energy. It is not recommended placing a mirror opposite a front door, as it reflects the good energy back out of the house.*

The ancient Chinese method of Feng Shui helps us to balance our homes and create happier, more successful lives.

There are many books and advice on the Internet that can help you to create good Feng Shui in your home.

Displays of fresh flowers and plants promote positive energy, although anything with thorns should be avoided. A bowl of fruit rather than flowers in the bedroom is supposed to encourage sexual health, and displays of oranges and lemons throughout the home are thought to bring good luck.

A water feature is key in the successful implementation of **Feng Shui** principles, which translates as "wind water". A water feature will promote feelings of relaxation and harmony.

Colours have a special significance, with different colours representing different things. Green symbolises nature and therefore represents life and hope, yellow represents power and red and purple are said to be lucky. Relaxing colours are best used in living spaces.

Avoid sharp lines and corners, as they emit negative energy. Wherever possible corners should not point to beds or chairs as they will prevent calmness and relaxation.

If you wish to look into this further there are many books and advice on the Internet that can help you to create good **Feng Shui** in your home. You may not be able to incorporate all the principles, but you will find plenty of advice on how you can counteract many of the possible negative effects.

Once you have decided on the look and feel for your home, take care over how this gets interpreted into the detailed choices you need to make about curtains, wallpaper and finishing touches. Don't run out of energy at this point, these decisions are vital to the success of your design scheme.

Ensure that your home reflects your tastes and style rather than just what happens to be fashionable.

Curtains have a great impact in a room and are an expensive item so choose carefully the look, style and feel that you desire.

There is more to curtains than choosing the fabric, the length, curtain heading and trimmings all have an impact on the final effect.

There are alternatives to curtains, there are blinds, shutters, screens and stained glass, which may be a better option.

Flooring is the hardest working surface of all therefore it is just as important to consider the practical aspects as the aesthetic ones.

Walls dominate a room in that they are probably the largest surface area on view and are probably where your choice of colour and pattern will dictate the overall style.

The choice of wall treatments is far greater than simply between paint and wallpaper, so investigate the alternatives before making a decision.

When choosing your finishing touches these should be given as much consideration as the rest of the interior design scheme.

More than anything else your choice of finishing touches is personal and specific to you and your family. This is the place to celebrate your individuality.

Feng Shui has principles, which explains how to organise your internal spaces to ensure the maximum flow of positive energy.

Understanding design principles

HOT TIPS

A final word

When I am creating interior designs for my many clients, there are things I do everyday that have become instinctive and natural, and it wasn't until I decided to set it all down in writing that I realised how much knowledge I use. I hope by sharing this knowledge with you, it will help you become more creative, better prepared and more confident to style your home.

A book on Interior Design can never be definitive - as the world changes so does the impact on our homes and therefore their design. I find I learn something new with each project, however the underlying principles remain the same. Investing time, money and energy well into your home will pay you back handsomely. Not only will you have created a beautiful and unique home for you and your family you will have increased its value as well. Restyling your home will take you on a journey of discovery, and although it may be at times frustrating, the end result will be worth it.

Keep your dreams in focus and enjoy the journey. Anything that is worth doing is worth doing well.

If you need any further assistance with your interior design project then please visit **www.designbydeborah.co.uk** where you can leave us a message and we would be very happy to help. You can also follow us on Twitter or Facebook at designbydeborah for regular design tips and blogs. Connect with us on Linked In or take inspiration from our Instagram and Pinterest boards.

We would love to hear from you.

www.designbydeborah.co.uk